Praise for

"Reading *Juicy Life* is akin to following a skilled wilderness guide through the landscape of our own psyche. With a delightful blend of playfulness and passion, adventure and depth, Andrea Anstiss guides us through the tangles and caverns of our life to discover the deep joy and meaning that is our birthright. This is one deep dive you don't want to miss!"
Dr Paris Williams, PhD
Mindful Somatic Trauma Therapist and author of *Rethinking Madness*

"Andrea Antiss's book is the spiritual medicine we need right now. The world is in a trance of self-destruction. Each one of us must come out of our own trance and return to this Juicy Life in order to begin the process of repair. Andrea's book is the joyous gift that shows us how."
Jinen Jason Shulman
Author of *The Nondual Shaman*

"In her book *Juicy Life: 8 Surprising Steps to Awaken Your True Self*, author Andrea Anstiss presents a clear, concise manual for self-transformation. She offers a treasure trove of techniques to identify the 'Tricky Traits' that prevent you from living your best life. This book is practical and useful – it provides many examples of ways to free yourself from old patterns and heal the difficulties that show up in relationships with partners, colleagues and family members. I highly recommend this book for therapists, seekers, and anyone interested in personal growth; it is a great gift to humanity."
Dani Antman
Energy healer, spiritual counsellor
Author of *Wired for God, Adventures of a Jewish Yogi*

"Andrea is a brilliant therapist and she shares her skills and insights with the reader in an easy-to-read, systematic way. Anyone could benefit from this wonderful book."
Deanna L Mulvihill, PhD, RN
Author of *The Development and Evolution of Rebonding of the Body*

"Andrea takes us on a journey full of zest to awaken our True Self and our Juiciness by acknowledging the Tricky Traits we've picked up along life's way. She alerts us to our strengths and enables us to delve deeply into our key relationships to discover the core of who we really are. She writes in a warm and comforting style and her book is brimming with useful exercises and strategies to complete the 8 steps to our *Juicy Life*."

Ruth I. Rusby, PhD
Author of *A Celebration of Breastfeeding*

"This book is an invitation to awaken to the stories woven into our being during childhood. It elegantly reveals that while the past remains unalterable, by examining our personal narratives we can write a new story, and change the trajectory of our lives. I highly recommend it to anyone seeking a fuller, richer life."

Anita Johnston, PhD
Author of *Eating in the Light of the Moon*

"Andrea Anstiss offers the perfect 'cookbook' for a *Juicy Life* – and the ingredients are already within us. With humorous reflection, insights and exercises, this book gives compassionate, empathetic, and practical guidance on how to find your True Self. The 'cake' that emerges is a reflective, protected and emotionally stable you – a 'you' with a *Juicy Life*, in love with the world and with yourself."

Regina von Flemming
Supervisory Board Member,
14 years CEO & publisher of *Forbes* and *Newsweek* Russia

"*Juicy Life* is much more than just a self-help book. Andrea has placed within this offering a compass and hundreds of guiding lights that support the reader not only to reach a deeper understanding of the Self but guide them to a place where Self is understood as part of the continuum of all. Her writing supports us to be more loving, more responsible and more responsive and to recognize ourselves as an illuminated thread on the tapestry of human experience. Andrea's genius is in knowing relationship as opportunity and love as medicine."

Samar Ocean Wolf Ciprian
Custodian of the Arvigo® Institute, Qoya Teacher and Tree Activist

"Truly captivating. I am deeply touched by the genuine sense of compassion that fills the entire book, making the complex tangible. A must-read!"
Samar Ajami
Teacher and Healer at A Society of Souls,
The School for Nondual Healing and Awakening

"*Juicy Life* is an inspiring and thought-provoking read that offers valuable insights and practical guidance on how to overcome life's challenges and live a more authentic and fulfilling life."
Maha Taibah
Founder of RUMMAN

"Are you ready to move beyond your Tricky Traits and trauma towards a more *Juicy Life*? This book is a must-have. The 8 steps towards healing are a great companion as you walk the journey of awakening to your brilliance and beauty. Moving through these enriching steps, Andrea supports the reader to fall truly, madly and deeply in love with themselves and their life."
MayBritt Searty
Therapist and Family Constellation Facilitator

"This book is an invaluable tool for every client (and *shhh!* every therapist too!). Clear and simple, this is the most unputdownable and practical self-help book I've read in years."
Siog Moore
Nurse and founder of Little Land Nursery

"This wonderful little book is a fabulous way to start digging into patterns from the past that keep us from living a full and satisfying life. Densely packed with information and probing questions, but very accessible and written in a friendly, non-judgemental voice, it's like having a therapist in the room with you. Take small bites and give yourself time to digest this slowly. I will be recommending this to clients."
Kali Martin
Marriage and Family Therapist, MA, CCHT, LMFT

"As someone who has read a lot of self-help books, I did not expect to enjoy this book as much as I did. Andrea manages to make very deep, potentially heavy material seem playful, relevant and inviting. Her style of writing is relaxed and warm and feels like a blanket that you wrap around yourself as you search your soul. If you are someone who is ready to let go of the 'Tricky Traits' that are holding you back from living the life you know you were destined to live, then this book is the education, lifeline and map to freedom that you're looking for. It holds your hand through the dark stuff so you can get to solid ground, no matter what you are struggling with. It is a one-stop shop. Andrea's wisdom and experience as a therapist comes through loud and clear but so does her warmth and substance as a person. If every client worked through this book, it might put us therapists out of business!"

Kas Ross-Smith
Eating Psychology Coach

"Andrea Anstiss, in *Juicy Life: 8 Surprising Steps to Awaken Your True Self*, skilfully takes the reader first through 7 steps in compassionately bringing awareness to one's 'Tricky Traits' or the challenging patterns that sabotage us. Her breadth of accessible tools and succinctly delivered theories accompany the reader in taking responsibility for and acting on these traits. We are then ready for Step 8: embracing and expressing our Juicy, True Self. Andrea's clear, organized, and relatable writing makes this an overall easy read. This is a must-read guide for all of us to get on claiming and living the authentic life we are meant to live – now!"

Cyntha Gonzalez
Transpersonal teacher, coach and bodyworker

"Stellar work! Andrea writes with powerful, thought-provoking insights into what makes us the people we are today. *Juicy Life* delves into the Tricky Traits that we have acquired over our lifetime and guides us along the path of becoming our True Self."

Niamh Kenny
Educator

Juicy Life

8 SURPRISING STEPS TO AWAKEN YOUR TRUE SELF

ANDREA ANSTISS

First published in Great Britain in 2023 by Springtime Books

Copyright © Andrea Anstiss 2023

All rights reserved. No part of this publication may be reproduced, stored in or introduced into a retrieval system, or transmitted, in any form, or by any means (electronic, mechanical, photocopying recording or otherwise) without the prior written permission of the publisher.

This book is sold subject to the condition that it shall not, by way of trade or otherwise, be lent, resold, hired out, or otherwise circulated without the publisher's prior consent in any form of binding or cover other than that in which it is published and without a similar condition including this condition being imposed on the subsequent purchaser.

ISBN: 978-1-915548-07-8

Every effort has been made to contact owners of copyrighted materials referenced in this book for permission to use such materials.

Reference to the Hoffman Process®, methods and techniques is made herein pursuant to the express authorisation of Hoffman Institute International, which reserves all rights. Materials fully describing the Hoffman Process, methods and techniques are available only through the Hoffman Institute subject to disclosure agreements.

The '9 Steps to Healing Childhood Trauma as an Adult' were written by Dr Andrea Brandt PhD, psychotherapist and author of *Mindful Aging* (2017).

Disclaimer
All names, locations and identifying features of the people in the case studies have been changed to preserve the anonymity of the people involved.

*This book is dedicated to Beryl, Geoff and Phil.
Thank you for making it all possible.*

CONTENTS

Foreword	xiii
A Word on Diversity	xv
Introduction	xvii

STEP 1: Recognise Those 'Tricky Traits' — 1
- Tricky Traits — 2
- Acting out Tricky Traits — 5
- Vicious Vortexes — 7
- Sara's story — 8
- Our human condition — 11
- Trauma responses — 13
- Luminous being — 13
- Deep Dive – Your Juicy life — 15

STEP 2: Recognise the Impact: Your Mother — 21
- Emotional blueprints — 22
- Mother themes — 25
- Deep Dive – Tricky Traits from Mum — 26
- Tricky Trait checklist — 29
- Creating space — 31
- Raw feelings letter — 32
- Sammi's story — 34
- Sticky Tricky Traits – embodied letting go — 35
- Re-mothering — 39

STEP 3: Recognise the Impact: Your Father — 43
- The role of the Father — 44
- Father themes — 45
- Deep Dive – Tricky Traits from Dad — 46
- Tricky Trait checklist — 48
- Creating even more space — 50
- Raw feelings letter — 51
- Anthony's story — 53
- Sticky Tricky Traits – embodied letting go — 55
- Re-fathering — 57

STEP 4:	Recognise the Impact: Your Ancestors	61
	Invisible ties that bind	62
	Your roots	64
	Everyone belongs	65
	Family Constellations group work	66
	A mysterious field	67
	Healing sentences	68
	Principles for restoring love	69
	Sibling strife	70
	Deep Dive – Your family system	72
	The family tree	75
	Amy's story	77
	Calling in your ancestors – a meditation	81
STEP 5:	Identify and Embrace the Trauma	85
	Embrace your trauma	86
	Trauma Traits	89
	Four Deep Dives about trauma	90
	Naming abuse	91
	The Three Bs	95
	Repair or repeat?	96
	Sunita's story	98
	Deep Dive – Nine stages of healing trauma	102
	Write your life	107
	The animal fable	107
STEP 6:	Create Your Boundaries	111
	Boundaries are your BFFs (best friends forever)	113
	Boundary bounty	115
	People-pleasing problems	116
	CoDA curious	119
	Deep Dive – Tricky Traits of co-dependency	120
	The nitty-gritty of boundaries	122
	Six pointers for healthy boundaries	127
	Empowered engagement	128
	Kareem's story	130

STEP 7:	Ditch the Toxic Shame	135
	Reactivity or receptivity?	136
	Oh shame!	136
	Shame sources	140
	Deep Dive – Befriending shame	142
	Stop the self-shaming	144
	Transforming shame messages – six questions	145
	Slippery shame	145
	Projecting light and darkness	148
	Tricky transference	152
	Deep Dive – Growing yourself back up	156
	Sina's story	158
STEP 8:	Embrace the Juicy Life	163
	Your unrepeatable loveliness	165
	Deep Dive – Receiving grace from Mum and Dad	168
	Deep Dive – Receiving grace from your culture	170
	Wonder child	171
	The upside of your Tricky Traits	172
	Steve's story	173
	Embodied ecstasy	174
	Who am I?	177
	More than you here	180
	Everyone is accountable and no one is to blame	182
	Towards understanding and compassion	184
	Moving on	187
	And finally… the power of a cosmic giggle	187

Resources   *191*
Appreciation   *197*
About the Author   *200*

FOREWORD

I remember the time my sons were teenagers, spending hours on their mobile phones, when I would try every argument to get them to pick up a book instead. My final tactic was to say, "Look, in one book you get the wisdom of someone's whole life. Imagine how much that can help you figure things out." That actually did get their attention and now in their mid-20s they are regularly spotted with a book in their hands, to my continual but pleasant surprise.

This is one of those books that I would love them to read. In it a supremely skilled therapist, who has lived in the Middle East for many years and knows its culture intimately, collects her learnings from a lifetime of travels and studies. Here you will find the very best of what there is to offer from many traditions and methods. The result is a handbook of how to navigate life with a series of eight clearly defined and very attainable steps.

I worked closely with Andrea for a number of years in the Hoffman Institute, so I know at first-hand how deeply she has explored the ways to uproot any family conditioning that might be holding us back. Starting with that firm foundation, she then goes on to include family constellations and the legacy of further generations back. As if that itself were not enough, she then puts her laser focus on any trauma and shame that could still be slowly releasing their toxins into our lives. But know that although these are profound and sometimes scary subjects, we are reminded with humour and appreciation that each of us has what Andrea calls a True Self. That is the part that is worth rediscovering, the buried jewel that allows us to live a juicy life.

In her practice Andrea is continually working with people suffering from deep trauma and yet remains one of the most upbeat people I know. With her contagious laughter always at the ready, she truly 'walks her talk' as a beacon of light spreading a message of love and positivity in a world that so needs this kind of work.

May her message as clearly spelled out here spread to you, your family and community so we can do all we can to change ourselves and those around us. Through that, may the world be left in a better place than it is now.

Tim Laurence
Founder and Director, Hoffman Institute UK
Author of *You Can Change Your Life*

A WORD ON DIVERSITY

Throughout the book, I will be assuming an extended and nuclear family system and will therefore refer to 'Mum' and 'Dad' and other traditional familial roles within that system. This is for the sake of ease of writing and is in no way meant to exclude those of you who were raised in families with a different system in place or with primary caregivers who were not your biological parents. For instance, particularly in the Middle East, a lot of children are raised – at least in part – by nannies of different cultural backgrounds. Sometimes this attachment is primary. It can be similar for children who are raised by a grandparent. It is also in no way meant to exclude those of you who may have been raised by non-binary parents, parents in same-sex partnerships, single-parent families, blended families and the myriad of different variations of the family system. I would encourage all of you to see the reality of the feminine and masculine principles within us all and to see that mothering and fathering are energies that can come from various sources. So, when I refer to 'Mum' or 'Dad', please do replace those words with the names of whoever was responsible for giving you nurturing and care when you were a child.

INTRODUCTION

> "Paradise is not a location; it is not part of the geography.
> Paradise is a certain attitude towards existence;
> it is a way of life."
>
> Bhagwan Shree Rajneesh

You are a multidimensional being on a remarkable and courageous journey of discovery and evolution. Your presence on the planet is a result of many complex relationships coming together. Your precious presence is born of your ancestors who came long before you and ancient stars who lent you the elements to form your physical body.

As of yet, you may feel unaware of your multidimensionality. You may even be unhappy that you have a physical body at all, resentful that you are here on this blue-green playground with other humans. It may seem as if an innate sense of Joy has divorced you or perhaps was never yours to begin with. Perhaps you feel stuck in patterns that feel impossible to either accept or change. Hopefully you have some vague memories of delighting in life before the burdens of the world slunk heavily across your shoulders and burrowed into your guts.

The mission of this book is to help you to uncover and recover your 'Juiciness' and be seated in what I like to call your True Self. So, what is your True Self and why is it not shining brightly, illuminating you and the world?

YOUR TRUE SELF

There are hundreds of descriptors for your spiritual being: your essential self, your inner light, your spiritual self and your higher self, to name a few. I will often refer to your spiritual self as your 'True Self'. Your True Self informs how your being shows up in the world as you; with your form, your individuality and richness.

The difficulty we all face is to stay connected with our True Self. We lose connection with it as we fall into the limited stories – or what I call 'Trances' – created by our unconscious negative conditioning. Our Trances are based on our unexamined past. Our limited stories or Trances are made up of clusters of troublesome or negative patterns; I refer to these as 'Tricky Traits'.

The big Trances I see many of my clients ensnared in are the Trance of unworthiness and the Trance of unlovability. Many people also live in the Trance of shame. For your True Self to shine with all its Juiciness and light, these limited stories about who you imagine yourself to be deserve to be questioned. To truly challenge our limited programming, to break the Trance, we need to thoroughly investigate the roots of our conditioning, including our trauma. We need to be willing to see clearly how our family lineage has impacted us.

FAMILY SOUP

One of the biggest influences in your life today is the relationship you had as a child with your parents or early caregivers. From these major players and family members, you have learnt key ways of feeling, thinking and behaving. Much of what you learnt from your upbringing may have served you well. From conception to around the age of seven, we all absorb information from our environment like a piece of pasta floating in minestrone soup; the flavour of that soup is determined by our parents' attitudes, behaviours, moods and rules. From our time in the womb until we leave home, we are steeped in our Family Soup.

Many of the Family Soup flavours have been passed down from previous generations. The flavours have been influenced by the cultures our ancestors grew up in. The soup you grew up in was also influenced by larger forces: the trauma your ancestors experienced and the trauma you experienced. Some of the patterns we have inherited from our ancestral lineage are quite hidden. This is why we need to find the courage to dive deep.

It's helpful to remember that there was at least some nourishment in your particular Family Soup. After all, you are still breathing and here today. Right this moment, I invite you to take a deep breath in and a long slow breath out. Yes, breathe.

As little ones, we often take on feelings, beliefs and attitudes that are now well past their sell-by dates. These Tricky Traits may be shrouding your Joy and expression of your True Self; they may be preventing you from being a thriving human in this post Covid-19 era. When our Juiciness and True Self are buried under a pile of difficult patterns, we have work to do. That's what I'm here to help you with.

> "Remember to delight yourself first, then others can truly be delighted."
>
> Sark

AWAKENING TO TRICKY TRAITS

In order for you to connect with Joy and Juiciness in your life, I invite you to consciously choose to awaken to the Tricky Traits you internalised as a child.

Criticism is an example of a classic Tricky Trait that creates struggle and pain for us. We may have learnt to be critical because we heard our mother criticising our father or her friends:

"Your father is such a disaster with money!"

Or we experienced criticism directly from our mother:

"Oh Fatima, you're hopeless at maths, and why is your room *always* such a mess?"

Because we depend upon our parents' attention for survival, we adopt their behaviour. We become like them in the hope they will accept us and give us the attention, physical closeness, food and shelter that we instinctively know we need in order to survive.

Classic Tricky Traits

To help you understand what a Tricky Trait is, here's a short list. I have given you examples that I often see my clients wrestling with. Do you recognise any Tricky Traits here that may be in the way of you connecting to your True Self and expressing your Juiciness?

* I'm not good enough.
* I'm wrong.
* I'm not as intelligent as the others.

- Poor me.
- I'm not wealthy.
- I'm impossibly stuck in my hopelessness.
- I'm addicted to alcohol/food/work/sex/seeking/suffering.
- I hate my body.
- My trauma history is who I am.
- My life is shit.
- Nothing works.
- I'm alone and lonely.
- I don't belong.
- I'm a disaster at relationships.
- The planet is f**ked and so am I!

ROCK SOLID RESOURCES

In exploring your inner landscape and becoming aware of your Tricky Traits, I want to remind you of the skills and strengths you already have within you. These resources will support you on your journey. Knowing you have some of these resources will make you feel safer about entering into the wilderness of your Tricky Traits.

These strengths include your agency or power, your kindness, your sense of adventure and your ability to laugh. You wouldn't have picked up this book if you didn't have a sense of adventure. Bear in mind that these positive resources form part of the positive inheritance – that is, the good stuff – you received from your Family Soup. Let me elaborate on these inner resources further.

Adult agency

As infants and small children, we have very little agency. And now, because we are smart, we know that it is neither our role nor our responsibility to change our parents (not that it is even within the realm of possibility to change them). We can, however, seize the opportunity to transform ourselves. As adults we have that freedom. And with freedom comes the opportunity for self-responsibility. Freedom and self-responsibility go hand in hand.

We now have the power to free our inherent Juiciness and the discernment to identify and choose fresh beliefs, attitudes and feelings that actually serve us. We can release the Tricky Traits that don't nourish our Joy.

> "What we call personality is often a jumble of genuine traits and adopted coping styles that do not reflect our true self at all but the loss of it."
>
> Gabor Maté

Attitude of adventure

It is important to leap into exploring our Tricky Traits with a sense of adventure. The 8 Steps in this book open up a journey into the deepest corners of your own beautiful and challenging inner landscape. As you complete the Deep Dives in this book – experiences to help you explore the intimate details of your past and how it impacts your present – you will become skilled at exploring your Tricky Traits. Looking at the difficult patterns of our early history that are still alive in us today can be both a thrilling and a confronting ride. Yet taking responsibility for uncovering the Tricky Traits that have been running our lives is our ticket to freedom.

There is magnificence in connecting to and expressing our spirit. The centre of who we really are is where our True Self resides but is shrouded by our Tricky Traits. Our Tricky Traits work collectively as a story or script that we unconsciously act out in our lives. When we carry out this script or conditioned story, we are in a Trance. Trances create separation from our core goodness, from our Juiciness and from others. They stop us from celebrating the privilege of being alive on this extraordinary planet, with all its problems, promise and beauty.

Resistance

It takes heart and guts to recognise and dive into acknowledging our Trances. We need to be willing to shine the light of our awareness on what may feel murky or even dangerous. There exists in our beings a certain resistance to awakening and evolving. It takes commitment to challenge our Trances. The English writer and philosopher Alan Watts called it the "taboo against knowing oneself". When you hit your resistance, don't resist it further. Instead, remember to be kind to yourself and go gently.

Kindness

Traits are tricky because they can ambush us when we think we finally have all of our shit together. Confronted by my partner Phil's recent illness, I have been observing a distinct irritation rise in me when concerns over his health dominate much of our conversation. I have also noticed feeling numb and removed from him and the present moment.

As I began to witness these Tricky Traits in myself, I was able to trace them back to the ways my parents sometimes dealt with illness and loss when I was young. For instance, my mum had experienced much loss in her life by the time she had me, in part because her own mother suffered from TB and passed away when Mum was only 21. Her sense of overwhelm was passed on to me when I was little. By making the connection with this early conditioning and understanding why Mum would have felt so overwhelmed in the face of loss, I have been able to meet my conditioned Tricky Traits of irritation and numbness with kindness. This allows me to connect to and feel the deep sadness inside of me about Phil's illness and to open my heart to both of us.

Humour

Humour is often present where there is kindness. The ability to laugh at ourselves and our human predicament is wonderful medicine. Laughing at ourselves and our Tricky Traits can be a shortcut to our Joy. Sometimes laughter taps into tears, and tears are welcome too. All of your feelings are welcome.

The way to healing is the full expression of your feelings. This includes great uproarious belly laughs that I have often seen after my clients have expressed grief. As you work through the Deep Dives in this book, I invite you to allow space for all your feelings to move and flow. We don't want to use humour to avoid our pain, but laughing at ourselves and life is seriously important!

> All of your feelings are welcome

Spaciousness

Self-kindness is essential as you journey through the experiences in these pages. Your Tricky Traits are like a haze covering your True Self and Juiciness. As we become aware of our Tricky Traits and transform them, we create more space in our bodies and minds. This spaciousness is a result of kindness towards ourselves and our human conditioning.

Spaciousness happens as we release judgement of ourselves and others. Spaciousness occurs as we let go of the identities that no longer serve us. In this spaciousness there is more room for our Joy to shine forth.

Tricky Traits do not define you. They are not your real identity. Your True Self, in all its radiance, has been here all the time but cloaked by clusters of these negative, difficult traits.

We could visualise your True Self as the sun and your Juiciness as the rays. But the false stories, which I call Trances, created by the conglomeration of Tricky Traits, have shrouded the sun. You are out of connection with who you really are. Without taking action, you become overly identified with your collection of Tricky Traits. Often my clients speak of feeling lost. They have lost touch with their True Self, their Joy and their Juiciness.

> Tricky Traits do not define you

In creating more spaciousness in your life, you have room to invite in what *you* truly want to have, do and be. Your life and your place in it need no longer be determined by the Tricky Traits of your family. In *Step 1*, you will define what you really want in your life. This will fuel your motivation for taking action and engaging in the Deep Dives.

THE THREE INNER STEPS

There are millions of ways to transform and awaken, and there are zillions of models, workshops, books and YouTube videos about how we might do this. One of the models I love is adapted from the work of Dr Christine Caldwell, a somatic psychology professor who developed a therapy called The Moving Cycle. The Moving Cycle has four phases: awareness, owning, appreciation and action. In this book, I have simplified the four phases to three – three 'inner steps' you will take as you engage with each Deep Dive:

1. AWARENESS: Become *aware* of the thoughts in your head and the feelings and sensations in your body. Notice them. *Awareness* is an act of self-kindness.
2. OWNING: Know that these are your own thoughts, feelings and sensations, and it is up to you to transform them, even though you learnt them from others. Although these Tricky Traits did not begin with you, *owning* empowers you to take responsibility to change.
3. ACTION: Take the necessary *action* to change your old patterns and habits. Follow the 8 Steps and complete the Deep Dives. As you connect with your Joy, allow yourself to act and express your True Self more and more. Through *action* we take our awakening and our Juiciness to the streets where we can light the way for all.

Please hold the inner steps in mind as you engage with the Deep Dives in this book. I strongly invite you to commit wholeheartedly to the Deep Dives and experiences I offer you. Without participating in them – with your journal and pen in hand or your writing device at the ready – you are short-changing yourself (in fact, short-changing yourself may be the first Tricky Trait you wish to identify and challenge).

The questions I ask you in each Deep Dive are designed to pique your curiosity and increase your self-knowledge. By journaling your responses to the questions and paying attention to your habitual feelings, sensations, thoughts and behaviours, you will increase your awareness.

Simply by becoming more aware of your Tricky Traits, you begin to metabolise and transform your patterns. This is what taking ownership is all about.

Also, be sure to *do* some of the 'embodied letting go' experiences I have outlined in *Step 1* and *Step 2*. Action is imperative. Appreciation and celebration of your being will organically arise as you engage with all the Steps in this book.

'NOT ENOUGH' DISEASE

Our Tricky Traits can collectively create 'not enough' or 'deficiency' Trances. We are hypnotised into believing these Trances are true and act as if they are. In our Trance, we live in a kind of social amnesia; we forget we belong to this enormous human family. We feel disconnected, separate from peace and from the Joy that allows us to celebrate life. In a Trance, we also feel like the party is happening somewhere else! We imagine Juiciness only exists outside of ourselves. This sends us into 'seeker' mode, where we miss the moment and are forever looking for the next:

* Teacher
* Therapist
* Guru
* Movement/church
* Coach
* Face or plastic surgeon
* Body or personal trainer
* Workshop
* Book
* Addiction to dull the pain – drugs/thrills/sex/holidays…
* New 'thing'

Now is the perfect time to claim your True Self and dance with all your Juiciness. What might happen if you fully enter the dance of your one precious life? What might happen if you do as the great mythologist and philosopher Joseph Campbell suggests and you "follow your bliss"?

STEP 1

RECOGNISE THOSE 'TRICKY TRAITS'

> "Dance when you're broken open.
> Dance if you've torn the bandage off.
> Dance in the middle of fighting.
> Dance in your blood.
> Dance when you're perfectly free."
>
> **RUMI**

In the coming chapters we will explore the influence of our key relationships and in doing so help identify and transform our Tricky Traits. These relationships include our primary caregivers, our ancestors, our trauma, our boundaries and our shame. But first, I want to help you become clearer about the troublesome or negative patterns I call Tricky Traits.

The reason I don't simply call them negative traits is because traits and patterns have a flipside. If we label something as negative or bad only, we don't leave space to see further. Often there are hidden resources enfolded in a particular Tricky Trait; we'll explore the flipside or the upside of your Tricky Traits in *Step 8*.

TRICKY TRAITS

So what is a trait? I worked for seven years for the Hoffman Process. This powerful residential workshop uses various techniques to help participants spot negative patterns. The Hoffman Process is designed for people who are "fed up of being fed up". Participants are often those in crisis: from divorce or illness to a business failure or major grief. A Hoffman Process workshop is a seven-day romp through and beyond multitudes of outdated, outmoded patterns and into real change. The process is cleverly designed to support you to identify your particular set of inherited negative traits, celebrate your inner child and move you out of a rut.

Defining Tricky Traits

The Hoffman Process defines a negative trait as any human behaviour, feeling or thought that takes you away from your authentic self. Tricky Traits block you from living your True Self. They are learnt, compulsive and automatic. Your Tricky Traits form the false stories – or Trances – you may be stuck in.

I listed some examples of Tricky Traits in the *Introduction*. Here are some more:

* Judging others and/or yourself
* Feeling less than others or superior to others
* Self-consciousness
* Worthlessness
* Criticising others and/or yourself
* Helplessness
* Passivity

To help you identify the Tricky Traits you may have absorbed from your early caregivers, take a look at the Tricky Trait lists in *Steps 2 and 3* (*Recognise the Impact: Mother/Father*). Please bear in mind that in *Step 8* we will focus on appreciating and harnessing the gifts you received from each parent too. Becoming *aware* of the Tricky Traits that stand between you and your True Self is the first step. With the support of the processes in this book, you will begin to clearly identify the Tricky Traits that are tripping you up.

> Becoming aware of the Tricky Traits that stand between you and your True Self is the first step

Four Tricky Trait sources

There are four main sources from which we form the Trances or false stories we act out in our lives. The Trances are formed on an unconscious level, and many of us are oblivious to the fact that we have been conditioned into thinking and feeling the way we do. We may believe 'Oh, this is the way I am and that is that'. When you are working on identifying Tricky Traits, it may be helpful to consider each of these possible sources:

1. *Modelling*
    Remember the adage 'Do as I say, not as I do'? It doesn't work that way for children. In watching and listening to how our parents and others behave, we learn how to respond to the world. If our parents' actions were inappropriate, ignorant or harsh, we took that modelling in. For example, if we had parents who were irresponsible with money, we may have learnt we didn't need to take care of our own finances – and suffer financial woes as a result.

2. *Rules and directives*
    These are statements that, as children, we hear as absolutes. Examples are: 'Don't cry, don't be sad' and 'It's unladylike to beat the guys and win'. One that many of us raised in the UK, Australia and New Zealand heard was, 'Don't show feelings'. Or worse still, 'Don't feel'. Rules often include 'shoulds'. For instance, 'You should be perfect' or 'You shouldn't be so upset'. Sometimes these rules and directives are not explicitly stated, but as children we hear them subliminally loud and clear.

3. *Labelling*
    These are direct, personal messages we receive from our caregivers and community about who we are. For example, 'You're spoilt', 'You're fat', 'You're disorganised', 'You're hopeless at sport'. We assimilate these labels and they direct how we see ourselves. If we are female and we hear our mother being labelled, by association, we also absorb that label. For example, if we witness someone

telling our mother 'You're incompetent and irrational', as her daughter, we may also absorb this judgement as though it were said directly to us.

4. *Suggestions*

These are subtler messages, sometimes delivered in the form of a declaration. Examples are: 'We don't want any artists in our family; they're too airy fairy', 'All the women in our family should look polished, no matter the occasion' and 'We come from a long line of Irish drinkers'.

ACTING OUT TRICKY TRAITS

Once we have absorbed the Tricky Traits of our caregivers, we play them out in three significant ways. They are: using the Tricky Trait towards ourselves, using it towards others, and finally, we unconsciously invite others to use the Tricky Trait towards us. Let's use criticism as an example of a universal Tricky Trait to illustrate this.

Three ways we engage with the Tricky Trait of criticism

1. Towards ourselves: we become self-critical. Most of us know how painful and destructive an inner critical voice can be to our feelings of lovability and preciousness.
2. Towards others: we may be critical towards our partners, whom we find intensely annoying and incapable of getting anything right. Or we may feel intense irritation towards our mothers-in-law, rage towards the neighbours or fury with politicians.
3. The third way we adopt Tricky Traits is a little more, well... tricky! We unconsciously set up the environment for others to do it to us. This usually happens below the level of our everyday awareness. We draw people to us who act our negative trait out against us.

They 'do it' to us. We may find ourselves with an employer or a partner who seems intensely critical.

'Rebel, Rebel'

As children, we had no choice but to take on the traits of our caregivers. This was an intelligent survival strategy. But often, as teens or young adults, we react to those original Tricky Traits by attempting to do the opposite. Part of our reason for doing that is the need to *individuate*, to discover who we are as beings separate from our parents. For example, if we had parents who emphasised extreme organisation and discipline, at some point we might want to escape the feeling of being controlled and do the opposite by becoming chaotic and messy.

Rebellion often creates a conflict between two opposing Tricky Traits. In the example above, there is the original trait of control and rigid organisation and the rebellious trait of messiness. Often, we feel caught between two traits and flip back into the parental trait of extreme organisation when we are stressed. Or we race between the two traits, 'Marie Kondo-ing' everything around us and then collapsing back to chaos. Unexamined rebellion can create anxiety and ambivalence. During times of stress or fear we usually propel back to the original trait. In rebelling, we put lots of energy into being different.

For example, if you were brought up by parents who were workaholics and demanded perfection, you are likely to have adopted this trait. But later in life you notice how tough you are with yourself and by comparison how much more fun your friends are having. You rebel by becoming a chilled-out drop-out who doesn't bother finishing their studies. This reaction has consequences for your self-worth and your ability to get a job and fulfil your potential. In rebellion we are attached to two Tricky Traits. In this example, the first trait is perfectionism and the second trait is laziness. When we rebel, the second Tricky Trait is often a reaction rather than a conscious choice. Rebelling can be useful as a teenager as we try out new ways of being, but if we are stuck in rebellion for years, it's both exhausting and inauthentic.

Sometimes we rebel to create some attention, especially if we were not given the attention we needed as children. For a little one or a teen, receiving negative attention is better than getting no attention at all. An example from my own life illustrates this well. My son's friend, Ali, whose parents were almost always busy with work, stole his dad's new Porsche convertible for a joy ride in the dead of the night. As Ali drove into the service station to refill the tank so his dad wouldn't be suspicious, he sideswiped another car. He succeeded in getting the negative attention of the police, the school and his neighbourhood. And, of course, his parents. This incident was a frightening wake-up call for Ali and his parents. His parents were smart enough to understand that Ali deserved a whole lot more attention and direction than he'd been getting, particularly from his dad.

VICIOUS VORTEXES

Individual Tricky Traits can work in teams. They hook up together, sucking us into a negative vortex of painful feelings, thoughts and behaviours. These traits feed each other. A vortex is created that has its own powerful momentum. You may also think of it as a 'negative cycle'.

An example of a Vicious Vortex is where our uncontained anger leads to dumping this aggression on someone. This creates guilt and perhaps shame also. Shame is such an uncomfortable feeling that we turn next to an addiction, such as drinking or overeating, as a strategy to avoid feeling the shame. We use our addictions to take us away from painful realities and difficult feelings. Our addictions act as numbing agents and are a symptom of deeper pain. Then we cycle back to feelings of anger and guilt again, or perhaps just into disgust at ourselves because of our addiction. Our anger was not given space to be expressed in a healthy way in the first place. Instead, it was leaked or dumped on another and then we used an addiction to try to hide from our anger, shame and pain.

In Sara's story below, there is a Vicious Vortex at play. I have mapped this to give you an example of a negative cycle and then upgraded it to a Virtuous Vortex to give you a visual of how you can find an exit from a negative cycle. I invite you to map your own Vicious Vortexes and then upgrade them to supportive cycles or Virtuous Vortexes.

VIRTUOUS VORTEXES

The way out of a Vicious Vortex is to find a supportive place to exit the old and familiar cycle. We map the Vicious Vortex and figure out a place to exit its power by choosing one thought, feeling or behaviour/action we could change. From that change, we can map a Virtuous Vortex where healthy thoughts, feelings and behaviours can nourish each other in a cycle that will serve us.

Sara's story

Sara, who I worked with for some months, is the daughter of a rage-aholic. Her dad was verbally aggressive and physically violent with her, her sisters and her mother. Sara understandably had a great deal of anger about the way she and her female family members had been treated. Her anger spilled out onto her work colleagues, especially at times of high work stress.

She would feel immense guilt and shame about her uncontained behaviour around her colleagues because she absolutely did not want to be like her dad. She knew what it was like to be on the receiving end of a barrage of verbal abuse, yet she found herself doing the same. (This is fully understandable since we tend to replay the troublesome patterns of our parents, unless we take conscious steps to do life differently and practise fresh attitudes and behaviours. Knowing this, it's easier for me to meet Sara's guilt and shame with understanding and compassion and model that for her.)

The guilt and shame she felt were so terrible that she habitually used food to run from these feelings. After a verbal episode at work, she would return home to binge on food she had ordered for delivery. She shoved in the food – which gave her no pleasure – and kept eating long after she was stuffed full. Her addiction to overeating to mask her shame simply added more shame.

We mapped out the Vicious Vortex she was caught in. Mapping out the vortex gave Sara some distance from her thoughts, feelings and behaviours. It made it clear how her anger feelings initiated the cycle. They led to destructive behaviours and shame feelings, which led to binge eating and hatred of her body. I helped her to express the rage in healthy ways so it wouldn't continue to poison her and explode over her colleagues. The anger release practices she used were daily Shaking or Kundalini meditation (see *Step 2*), attending my Holotropic Breathwork workshop and committing to thrice-weekly strength training sessions to connect with her power.

As she released both her past and current anger, she was able to begin practising assertiveness. She started checking in with her feelings and needs and asking others to help her meet those needs.

We worked to connect with the immense sadness her rage was actually protecting. Together, we mapped out a Virtuous Vortex similar to the one below so she could see clearly that there were a number of choice points at which she could disengage from the Vicious Vortex. The Virtuous Vortex mapping made it clear where she could use her adult agency and not continue the same behaviours as her dad.

Sara's Vicious Vortex

- Anger (Feeling)
- Verbal aggression at colleagues (Action)
- Guilt and shame (Feelings)
- Binge on food (Action)
- I'm fat, unloveable and filled with shame (Thoughts & feelings)

Sara's Virtuous Vortex

- Anger (Feeling)
- Movement, meditation to release anger (Action)
- Grounded and calm (Feelings)
- Eating when hungry, eating slowly, with pleasure and focus (Action)
- Respect: I respect my body. I'm willing to see myself as loveable (Thoughts & feelings)

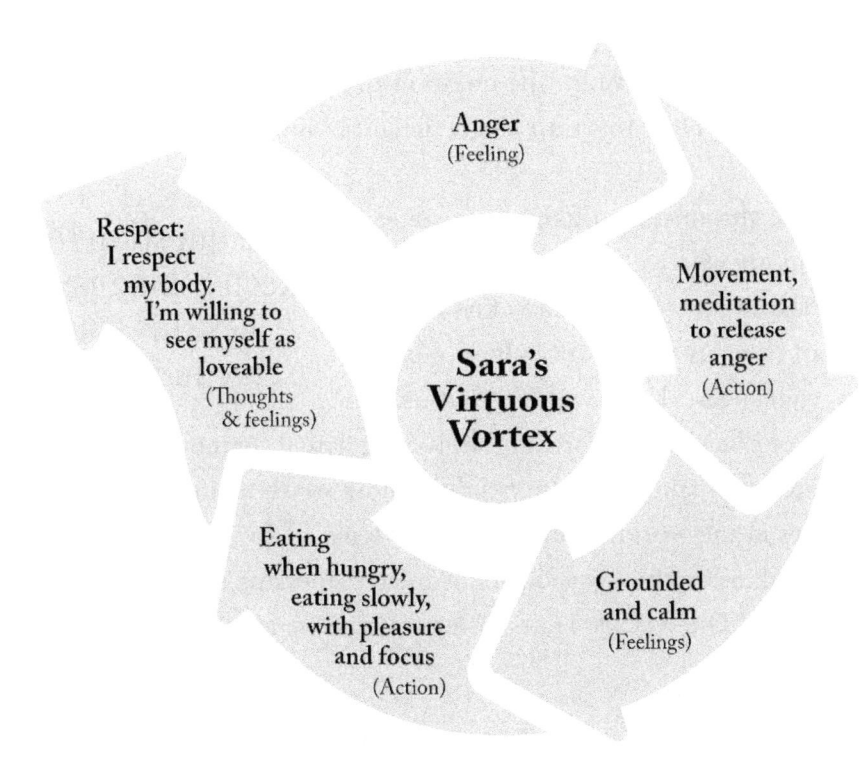

OUR HUMAN CONDITION

We need to be mindful of the fact that difficult traits are part of our human condition – and we each have many of them. Often we are unaware of our Tricky Traits because they seem so embedded in our way of being and have been with us for so long. They feel normal. They feel familiar. Often they feel comfy, like an old pair of slippers.

Complaining is an example of a trait that we may engage in without really noticing our behaviour. We take pleasure in whinging, moaning and fault-finding, perhaps with the waiter or the cleaning lady. Whole nations have become associated with this particular Tricky Trait. The 'Whinging Poms' stereotype comes to mind. Then there are the French who make being miserable seem charming! You don't have to give up complaining if you love it. The question to keep asking is, "Does this trait serve me? Does this trait create delight in my life?"

We make the mistake of thinking some of our traits are who we are. Out-of-date Tricky Traits that we have not yet awoken to are at the root of many of our difficulties: relationship challenges, how we feel about our bodies, our lack of self-care, and how we relate to money, work, sex, food and spirituality. They may inhibit how we show up and express ourselves in the world. They impact our sense of Joy in being here in our own skins on this gorgeous blue-green planet at a time of momentous change. Our Tricky Traits influence how we inhabit our lives.

> The question to keep asking is, "Does this trait serve me?"

Coping mechanisms

Again, it is essential to remember that we learnt these traits as children, often as a coping mechanism in a family environment that could not meet all our needs. We took on our parents' and caregivers' traits as a smart adaptation intended to keep us in the fold. We needed holding and touch, food in our bellies, a roof over our heads and some measure of human connection to survive.

Although we may not have been able to use words to speak, we adopted our parents' patterns as a plea or a bargain and were in effect saying: "Mummy, Daddy, I will become like you so you will love me, recognise me and keep me safe." It was a smart transaction but the reality now, as an adult, is that you may have a bunch of rules, beliefs, behaviours and feelings operating in your life that are not nourishing you and are certainly not serving your Joy or your deep connection to your True Self.

TRAUMA RESPONSES

We also adopted patterns in response to trauma in our environments, so some of our patterning may not have been learnt directly from our parents but rather as a survival response to a situation in our family, community or country.

Four Trauma Traits

The four big traits or patterns we may express as a result of trauma are:

1. Freeze
2. Flight
3. Fight
4. Fawn

For example, people who grow up in war-torn regions often have patterns of freeze that prevent them from feeling safe and connecting with their bodies and how they feel. Sometimes they may feel distanced from their bodies, out of rhythm with others and in a fog. I will invite you to explore your trauma responses in *Step 4*.

LUMINOUS BEING

You are a multi-layered, incredibly complex wonderling. (There is a therapy called Internal Family Systems, or IFS, that is based on the idea that we are made up of many parts or sub-personalities.) But to simplify, let's chop you up into just four parts.

Four parts

Essentially, these are the four parts that make us up:

1. *Feelings*

    Your feeling part is the same as your emotional part. Feelings are messengers about your reality. Your emotions are present even in utero. Most of the first five years of your life are experienced through your feelings. Our emotions connect to our bodies through our nervous system, our hormones and our water, including our tears and our hearts. Our feelings are where our experience in the world is processed and interpreted.

2. *Thinking*

    Our thinking part is our intellect or 'smarts'. Our thoughts, attitudes, prejudices and judgements are part of our intellects. This part includes our analytical thoughts, how we process information, how we learn at school and how we use our words.

3. *Physical*

    These are our bodies, including our skin and everything under our skin. Much of your work in tracking and releasing Tricky Traits is to help you become really comfortable in your own skin. Our body represents our physical experience in the world. And it houses our feelings, thinking and spirit. Our body registers sensations, important embodied messages about how we honestly feel.

4. *Spiritual*

    Our spirits are our connection to all things – including the earth and ourselves – and to what we call the universe, the divine, the higher self and what some call God. Our spiritual part provides us with protection, guidance and help. Your spiritual wisdom informs your True Self.

All of these parts of yourself are woven together to create the unique and rich fabric of your being. We divide them into parts to help you bring more awareness to who you are and how these parts interact.

In order for you to have the best time possible during your brief sojourn on earth, we want to invite your spiritual self to take a leading role. Your spiritual self permeates every part of your being. Your spiritual self is what guided you to read this book. It was present before you were born and it has never left you.

Your True Self is yours to unfold and radiate into the world. You are responsible for becoming intimate with it and then choosing to live informed by your light and not controlled by your traits. Let's revel in our light. In the next Step you will begin to identify any difficult Tricky Traits you took from your mum. But first, I want you to be radically honest about what you want for your life as you transform the Tricky Trait clutter. Clarity about what you want in your life will nourish your intention to complete all the Deep Dives.

DEEP DIVE
YOUR JUICY LIFE

Each of the Deep Dives in this book is designed to help you explore the intimate detail of your past and present. I invite you to bravely respond to the prompts and to journal the feelings, sensations, thoughts and insights that emerge.

This Deep Dive will help you discover what you want to do, be and have in your one precious life. How do you want to live your life? This is the time to think outside the box, outside your usual limitations. This is the space to feel into and consider what would be rich, Juicy and exciting for your life. Juicy for you may also mean simplifying your life. What have you never admitted to yourself that you would love to do, be and have because perhaps it seemed impossible, forbidden or cost too much? This is a time to be open, curious, to dream. Let your imagination be free and wild.

As you explore this and every Deep Dive, be conscious of your thoughts, feelings and sensations, remembering the three inner steps: *Awareness, Owning, Action.*

Have your journal or writing device ready and answer these questions. Remember to breathe deeply as you respond. Write spontaneously, not censoring or editing your words.

Let's start with broad brushstrokes. Imagine your best, most fulfilling life while you answer these general questions. Let your imagination take you wherever it wants to.

* What lifestyle do you have?
* What brings you Joy on a daily basis?
* What work are you doing?
* Who do you live with? Who do you see every day?
* What are you passionate about?
* How do you feel most of the time?
* Whereabouts are you in the world?

SUPER JUICY QUESTIONS

Now let's drop a little deeper into specific areas of your life. Again, envisage a life that you deeply love that celebrates your authenticity and precious presence.

Relationships
- How is your relationship with yourself? How is your self-esteem? What do you do for self-care? How do you renew your energy when you feel depleted?
- How are your relationships with your family? How often do you see them?
- How is your relationship with your partner(s)? What do you do for fun together? What does your partner most celebrate about you? How is your sex life?
- How are your relationships with your friends? How often do you see each other?
- How do your healthy boundaries express themselves in your relationships with yourself, your partner, your family, your friends? Are you able to say no when you need to?
- Who do you confide in?
- What gifts do you bring to your relationships?
- What does it feel like in your body when you imagine your tribe?

Physical wellbeing
- Imagine how you would love to be with your body. What does it feel like? How do you speak to each other?
- What do you notice about your energy in this Juicy life of yours? Are you aware of its ebb and flow?
- What about your sexual energy? How do you allow yourself to express and explore your sexuality?
- What is your relationship to movement? What exercise is the most fun for you?
- What is your relationship with food like? How does your intuition speak to you about food choices? What foods bring you the greatest pleasure? What about meal times? Do you sit down to eat? Light a candle? Do you like to chat as you eat?

* How do you look after your body? Do you take supplements? Do you get bodywork? Massage?

Emotional health
* How do you relate to your feelings? Do you welcome them all and allow your body to feel them fully? How do you allow them to flow?
* How well do you relate to your own heart and the passion and delight that lives there?
* What is your practice when it comes to emotional hygiene (this includes completing the unfinished business of your childhood)?

Work
* What kind of work or service would you love to be doing?
* How are your relationships with your colleagues and mentors?
* Where do you work? And how are your workspaces?

Wisdom
* Is there anything specific you want to learn, accomplish or grow?
* How do you feel or think about your intellect? How do you nurture it?

Finances
* How much money do you have?
* How is your relationship with money?
* What about savings, investments and philanthropy?

Location
* Where do you live?
* How are your living spaces?
* How is your relationship to Nature or the community in which you live?

Travel
- Are there places you would love to visit, explore or perhaps stay for a while?
- Are there cultures you want to experience and languages you want to learn?

Creativity
- How do you connect with your inner child or your freedom to express yourself and your feelings in creative ways?
- Are there creative channels you would love to explore, such as music or drama?

Spirituality
- How is your relationship to the mystery of life?
- What and how do you celebrate in your life?
- How is your relationship with beauty and awe?
- Do you want to cultivate more stillness?
- How are your spiritual practices?
- What delights you?

> "Change is inevitable,
> but transformation is by conscious choice."
>
> HEATHERASH AMARA

TLDR TOO LONG DIDN'T READ

If you're in a hurry or want a quick review of Step 1: Recognise Those 'Tricky Traits', here it is:

- (JL) You adopted difficult traits from your caregivers early on in your life.

- (JL) Those traits were taken on to gain connection with your parents so you could survive.

- (JL) Tricky Traits or difficult patterns are at the root of many of our challenges, including relationships, money, work, and health issues such as anxiety and depression.

- (JL) Tricky Traits can reinforce each other in Vicious Vortexes of thinking, feeling and behaviour.

- (JL) As an adult, you can choose to become conscious of those negative traits or remain stuck.

- (JL) Awareness is the first step.

- (JL) The truth is, you are your powerful spiritual self, or True Self. You deserve to connect to life from a place of Joy and Juicy possibility.

- (JL) Get super clear on what a Juicy life would be for you. This vision of your Juicy life will give you the rocket fuel to complete the 'Deep Dives' – experiences to help you explore the intimate details of your past and how it impacts your present.

STEP 2

RECOGNISE THE IMPACT: YOUR MOTHER

"When I stopped seeing my mother
with the eyes of a child,
I saw a woman who helped me
give birth to myself."

NANCY FRIDAY

As we begin to explore the influence of Mum (or your female caregiver), I encourage you to explore the difficult imprints that you took on from the mum of your childhood. You will identify the Tricky Traits you absorbed either directly or indirectly from her. Remember these Tricky Traits live in your head and nervous system and influence your feelings, attitudes and behaviours. You are looking for traits you absorbed from her. We call this the 'internalised' or 'introjected' mother.

We know that the mother of your early years is likely to be different from the mother she has evolved into now, decades later. If you are feeling protective towards your mum, be reminded we will return to her to honour the beautiful and powerful qualities you inherited from her, this woman who gave you life, in *Step 8*. While it's highly likely your mother did her best with you and your siblings, this work helps us to see that our early caregivers were human and flawed.

First, I encourage you to drop back into your childhood impressions and name the Tricky Traits that stand between you and your Joy in being alive and present. As you write your responses you will use your feelings and sensations to tap into your truth. Then you will choose from a menu of 'embodied' activities to support you in letting go.

EMOTIONAL BLUEPRINTS

We could consider emotions to be *energy + motion*. Emotions move through our body and if we have the courage to listen to our emotions, they provide us with essential information about our desires, our relationships and our environments. Our emotions orient us in the world. We connect with our emotions by checking in with them regularly. The attention we pay to our feelings correlates to the attention we were given as little ones.

If our mother noticed our sadness when we missed out on being chosen for the lead role in the school play and comforted us, we will be able to do the same for ourselves as adults. We will be able to meet our own difficult feelings with kindness. If instead she told us to stop that crying or she would give us something to really cry about, we learnt to be ashamed of our sadness and bury our hurt.

We were 'feeling beings' long before we became 'thinking heads'. We first experienced our universe via feelings and sensations experienced in our bodies, not through logical thought processes in the left hemispheres of our brains. This kind of thinking didn't kick in until we were around seven years old. A whole seven-year cycle of life had occurred before we began to think, and in those years, we were soft, permeable beings, literally absorbing the world around us. In the womb, as aquatic, feeling creatures, we experienced our mum's feelings, our dad's feelings and our environment. We took in how Mum felt about us, how she felt about Dad and how she felt about herself. Even today, we can access the feelings we had way back then. Notice what resonates with you or rattles you. Even if your feelings seem like faint whispers, trust them.

> If we have the courage to listen to our emotions, they provide us with essential information about our desires, our relationships and our environments

Adopted children

If you were adopted, you will need to look at the Tricky Traits you took on from both sets of parents: your biological parents and your adoptive parents. Even if you never met or know nothing about your biological parents, their traits have impacted you. Even if they had no other choice but to give you away, the patterns you have taken on from their trauma or Tricky Traits of abandonment or rejection deserve to be understood. You may, for example, feel a core sense of rejection, feel unlovable, disposable or worthless. It will be different for each person, so you will need to identify your particular Tricky Traits. You may also have adopted the pattern of rejecting – and do it to yourself and others. Or you may choose rejecting or abandoning people in your life and so set yourself up to be rejected again and again.

If you were adopted, I invite you to do the Deep Dives in *Steps 2* and *3* twice – once for your biological mother and father and again for your adoptive or foster parents.

The role of Mother

Now I want to invite you to become curious about the influence your mum had on the traits that create difficulties for you. As you read the themes and questions, notice where your mum may have overdone certain things, where her input was missing, or where she may have been neglectful. Become aware of the too much/too little places and how they may translate into your relationship with yourself and the world. Have your journal or note-taking app handy to jot down any insights.

You may want to protect your mum, but right now I want to support you in staying close to your own feelings and your precious heart. It's important to stay right next to the experiences you had, to understand what you learnt as a child and how that plays out in your life. Please use radical honesty about how you experienced your mother and how you took on patterned ways of being and negativity that now cloud your authenticity and Joy.

In reality, you could spend months exploring these key relationships with your parents. Remind yourself that the point is not to do this healing exploration perfectly but to identify the traits so you can restore the power of choice and delight in your life.

Four essential questions

As you identify a trait, ask yourself:

1. How was it as a child? Which Tricky Traits did I learn?
2. How is it now, acting out this trait?
3. What is the negative impact of this particular trait on my life?
4. Do I want to continue with this difficult pattern in my life or do I want to let it go?

MOTHER THEMES

Your mother's primary job was to nurture you. Reflect on these themes. How was she with you as a child? In some areas she may have been caring and supportive, but in other areas not so skilled. What did you learn from direct experience and her modelling? How are you with your own nurturance, care and respect?

- Love and accept
- Protect
- Respect
- Listen
- Guide
- Encourage
- Educate
- Teach boundaries

* Name feelings
* Play
* Model and mirror
* Be present

DEEP DIVE
TRICKY TRAITS FROM MUM

Journal your responses to these questions, listing any Tricky Traits you become aware of. The questions are derived from my teaching experience at the Hoffman Institute.

As you explore this Deep Dive into the traits you learnt from Mum, remember the three inner steps from earlier: *Awareness*, *Owning*, *Action*.

Take a few breaths. Allow your attention to move into your body. Get comfortable. As you sit, with your journal or writing device ready, feel the support of the cushions under you and behind you. Relax your shoulders. Soften any areas of tension. You are safe, and it's safe to know your own reality.

Gently take your imagination and awareness all the way back to the time of your conception. The questions will then lead you through stages of your life.

- What do you sense or know about your conception? Was your conception planned or a 'surprise'?
- What do you know about your time in the womb? The climate in the womb is impacted by our mother's emotional state and therefore affects the developing foetus. Even if you don't know any details, you may have a sense of how it was.
- Was your arrival into the world celebrated? Or do you feel you were born to serve another purpose, such as to fix the parental relationship, to replace a lost child or to bring honour or wealth?
- Did your mother spend time playing with you? Did she feel present?
- Did she guide you and teach you in a loving way?
- Did she encourage your desires and interests?
- Did she take the time to understand your point of view?
- Are you in relationships now where you feel discounted or unimportant?
- What were her messages about your body? Did she teach you that your body is worthy of respect and care no matter what?
- How was she when you were ill? Did she take care of you or were you sent to school anyway? Was it the only time she gave you attention?
- Did she have challenges with her own body image? What did you see or hear her say about her body?
- How was she around sex education – awkward or open?
- How was she with your changing body as you moved through puberty – did she prepare you for coming into womanhood/ manhood?
- How is your relationship with your own body a result of what your mother taught you, either directly or indirectly?

* And food – were you forced to clean your plate? Was there enough food?
* How were mealtimes with your family – relaxed, or silent and full of tension?
* And, as a result, how is your relationship with food? Friendly, or are you at war?
* How was she with discipline? Was she a 'jellyfish' mum, lacking in boundaries and follow-through?
* Was she fair or did she use harsh or even cruel punishment?
* Did she stand up for you? Did she protect you?
* How are you with self-regulation and self-discipline?
* What about school – were your achievements a way to get her attention?
* Did she support you with your projects?
* Did she celebrate your academic, creative and sporting successes?
* How do you value yourself? Do you only value yourself according to your achievements?
* If you were an 'expat' or military child or you moved places often, how did she support you with these transitions?
* How do you handle change in your life today?
* How was she with her feelings? For instance, was she depressed, violent or prone to playing the victim? Was she self-critical? A martyr?
* Is she an unhealed survivor of trauma or abuse? If so, in what ways did she pass this on to you?
* Was she an addict, using overeating, alcohol, drugs or other substances to seek the next high or numb her pain?
* How are you like her or how have you rebelled?
* Do you have to walk on eggshells around her?

- How are you with your own feelings? In what ways is your self-regulation similar to your mother's?
- What about her relationship with your father? What did she model around relationships with men? For instance, did she nag him or emasculate him? Did she complain about him to you, enlisting you as her friend, therapist or go-between?
- How do you relate to men? Is it possible that your views of men are informed by hers?
- What was her relationship to money? Was she frugal or generous? Did she earn her own money?
- Was she satisfied in her role as a homemaker or was she focused on her career? Was she a workaholic, with little time for you?
- What is your relationship like with money? Are you ever satisfied?
- If there was any kind of abuse happening in your family, did she ignore it, permit it, support it or even blame you for it?
- What impact did this have on your ability to trust life and set boundaries?

TRICKY TRAIT CHECKLIST

As you responded to the Deep Dive you will have identified a bunch of Tricky Traits. Here's another list of traits to support you in detecting those you learnt from your mother. Check if you experienced any of this kind of hurt or trauma, how it impacted you and how you may now do it to yourself or others. Look at how your mum may have acted out these traits but also where she couldn't or didn't protect you from others.

This list was inspired by Charles L. Whitfield, MD, who wrote many recovery classics, including *Healing the Child Within*:

Abandonment
Abuse of any kind
(*physical, mental, emotional, sexual, spiritual*)
Belittling
Betraying
Breaking promises
Bullying or overpowering
Controlling
Criticising
Cruelty
Deceiving
Disapproving
Discrediting
Disgracing
Dismissing
Humiliating
Inflicting fear
Inflicting guilt
Intimidating
Invalidating
Joking about or teasing
Laughing at
Limiting
Making vague demands
Manipulating
Misleading
Patronising
Responding inconsistently
Stifling
Withdrawing
Withholding love

CREATING SPACE

After identifying difficult feelings, thoughts and beliefs, including injustices and resentments, the invitation is to feel them, grieve them and release them. We want to create space between the Tricky Traits you adopted and your beautiful essence, spiritual self, or True Self. Your True Self is the wellspring/primary source of your Joy and delight. With this work, you are creating a whole new relationship with those Tricky Traits. Written expression and physical expression are great tools to use your strength as an adult and to honour the vulnerability of your child within.

Many of us came from families where the rule was to avoid expressing painful or difficult feelings. Our angry and hurt feelings went underground, along with our Joy. Often we don't know how or what we feel until we write or speak our thoughts and feelings.

In the letter-writing process outlined next, you will have an opportunity to write your truth. Allow yourself to access your heart, your vulnerability and your child within as you write. There may be many feelings not included in the list below. Please ad-lib and express your emotional truth. For example, the young part of you may resonate with other difficult feelings: you may feel hopeless, lost, frozen, stupid, terrified, overwhelmed, out of control, humiliated, shattered, lonely... the list of possible feelings is long.

The Feelings List on my website (andreaanstiss.com/juicylife) may help you identify and name your feelings. These are feelings we may not have been able to name or express because we were too young to know the words or because we were discouraged from expressing them. Use the words that fit for you.

You may want to change the stem sentences to write in the past tense. For example, it may be easier to connect with your unacknowledged feelings if you write "I felt angry" or "I was angry" rather than "I feel angry". Using the past tense "I felt…" may support you to access the voice of that little child within. Experiment with the raw feelings letter and discover what works for you.

RAW FEELINGS LETTER

Using the information you have just uncovered, you will write your feelings in a letter using the 'expressive letter' format. This format is inspired by John Gray's love letter process. John Gray is a relationship therapist who wrote the mega bestseller *Men Are from Mars, Women Are from Venus*.

Writing out our feelings with the intention of releasing them is a useful tool for letting go of our stale stories, stuck feelings and historical grief. Letting go opens the door to delight.

I encourage you to use this letter-writing format for all the mother figures who may have contributed to your Tricky Traits: stepmothers, aunties, nannies, female principals and teachers. These letters (you may need to write several) will never be sent, so it's a safe and contained way to acknowledge and release difficult feelings. Use the prompts to complete sentences that express your true feelings.

> **Letting go opens the door to delight**

Dear Mum or significant caregiver,

I am writing this letter to share my feelings with you:

For Anger

I don't like it
I feel frustrated
I am angry that
I am resentful that
I feel annoyed
I wanted
I want

For Sadness

I feel disappointed
I am sad that
I feel hurt that
I wanted
I want

For Fear

I feel worried
I am afraid
I feel scared
I am anxious that
I don't want
I wanted
I want

For Regret

I feel embarrassed
I am sorry
I feel ashamed
I don't want
I wanted
I want

Sammi's story

Sammi is the eldest daughter of a wealthy Lebanese family. Only a few days after her birth, both her parents flew to another continent where the extended family's businesses were based. Sammi did not connect with her mother again until she was a year old: she was left in the care of nannies and an elderly grandmother. When, eventually, she lived with her parents again, much of her mother and father's time was taken up with social engagements. Sammi continued to be left behind with the nannies and at eight years old was 'dropped' at boarding school. Her sense of abandonment was acute and palpable. The circles under her eyes were deep and purple, and her head bowed forward into her sunken chest. She was suffering from depression and chaotic eating, and she had very little sense of self despite being a wonderful artist. Her Joy had disappeared long ago.

The most difficult trait she adopted from her parents was abandonment, which she replayed as self-abandonment. Just as her mother had not been present for her feelings or her growing pains, Sammi found it extremely difficult to be present for her own feelings, pleasure and talents. We worked together for several sessions before she felt ready to engage in the letter-writing process outlined above. As she began the writing process, to her mother first, she realised there were others who had treated her unfairly. She wrote several 'love letters' to her uncle, who had been verbally aggressive to her as a teenager. She also identified a boarding school teacher who was particularly cruel. She then conscientiously engaged in two of the expressive practices outlined below.

Spontaneous painting was her favourite way of expressing her feelings. She bought huge canvasses and painted to empty each and every feeling out of her body onto the canvas. She splattered her tears and threw her resentment and her disconnection into her paintings. While the end product was never the purpose of her painting therapy, her paintings were spectacular. When she felt ready for another round of releasing the hurt caused by the abandonment, she danced. She created incredible playlists and sometimes danced on top of her paintings. Occasionally, she ripped up paintings and set them alight to release her rage at having been left at such a young age.

Through painting and movement she began to open up her heart and notice that some people in her life were consistent and trustworthy. She connected with her passion for design, pottery and painting. She was invited to exhibit her pottery and sculpture at local community centres and cafés. Today, five years after we first met, she is a radically different woman. She travels the tropical beach resorts of the world, blogs about her adventures, volunteers at a community art studio and creates stunning sculptures on commission.

STICKY TRICKY TRAITS – EMBODIED LETTING GO

Sometimes simply seeing our Tricky Traits is enough to begin to metabolise and change them. Awareness begins the transformation process. Sometimes we need to take more action because some traits are deeply ingrained, or 'sticky'. Tricky Traits have a life further afield than our head. They live in our body and we need to engage our body to transform them. In *Eastern Body, Western Mind*, Anodea Judith brilliantly describes how yogic philosophy views Tricky Traits as morphing into our issues, which are stored thematically at different energy centres in our body. For example, around our heart, we store themes relating to love, relationships and self-acceptance. The Tricky Traits that live here include unexpressed sadness, poor boundaries, possessiveness, loneliness, isolation, bitterness and criticism.

Embodied letting go – six experiences

We hold beliefs and feelings literally in the tissues of our body, so engaging our bodies in movement and expression is key. As you move, breathe deeply and feel into your body, I invite you to allow sounds and words to also move through and out of your throat.

There are so many creative ways to let go of Tricky Traits and create more space. Writing is a great start, but let's dive deeper into six ways you can use your body and breath to physically let go of Sticky Tricky Traits. You don't need to do all of these – just choose one or two that sound appealing.

1. *Dance*

    Write the Tricky Trait on a large piece of paper. Put on loud, percussive music. You can use Spotify or other platforms to find drumming music, tribal music and world music that has a strong beat. You'll find a link to one of my movement playlists on my website (andreaanstiss.com/juicylife).

    Move your body on the paper. Stamp, crush, rip and tear the paper with your feet. Or with your hands. Destroy that Tricky Trait. In places where you feel the sensations of that trait caught in your body, follow your impulse and move your body in ways that are freeing. For example, the Tricky Trait of carrying other people's problems often results in burden and heaviness around the shoulders and neck. The invitation is to pay attention to the heavy, tight or numb parts of your body and move in ways that loosen them. This may include making sounds. Breathe deeply.

2. *Movement*
Write the Tricky Trait on a small piece of card. Slip it inside your running shoes. Run hard using your legs, arms and lungs to release this pattern from your being and leave it in your trail. Or go to the gym and dedicate your iron pumping session to muscling out a couple of Tricky Traits.

3. *Shaking*
This is also known as Kundalini shaking. Put on dance music you love. Then simply shake your body. Shake your arms, your legs, your torso and your head. Be sure to shake your hips and pelvis, as this is where Sticky Tricky Traits related to our sexuality love to hide out. After a while your body takes over and begins to shake itself free. This is the wonder of our body's innate wisdom. The Osho Kundalini meditation is a great guide to shaking (see *Resources*).

I recently had an extraordinary experience with a plant medicine that activates the Kundalini shaking in the body. My body shook and trembled spontaneously for hours from the inside out! All the pain, rigidity and ancient fear were propelled out of my legs, particularly my knees, as I was simultaneously rocketed into the light!

4. *Breathwork*
Join a breathwork session, ideally in person with the facilitator.

If this is not possible then you can connect online. Use your body, your connected breath and the awesome soundscape to release what is no longer serving you. Holotropic Breathwork® is one of my favourite forms of breathwork as it allows for a three-hour experience of an expanded state of awareness. In this expanded state, we are able to access and release imprints that are normally below our everyday consciousness. For example, we can pick up on information from around our time of conception, time in the womb and early years – things that still impact us today.

Holotropic Breathwork, created by psychiatrist Stanislav Grof and his wife Christina, is just one of several breathwork modalities I have had the privilege to study and facilitate. *Hawa* Breathwork is another. *Hawa* is an Arabic word for wind and specifically a wind that carries our longing to return home. Our breath, used in a particular way, connects us to our inner wisdom and helps us to move through and beyond embedded patterns and into our True Self.

5. *Painting*

Grab some big pots of water-based paints and some big brushes. No brushes? Then use your hands and feet. Set your intentions around the traits you want to release. Use your non-dominant hand, which bypasses your 'inner critic', and paint onto large sheets of paper. Paint spontaneously, allowing your body to lead. The purpose is to release, not create something to hang on the wall. Remember to breathe fully; your outbreath will help you let go. Choose the colours that call to you. If you are wanting to release anger or rage, you might find yourself wanting to cut up or rip up the painting after. Do it!

6. *Voicing*

    As children we were usually not allowed to say no to our parents. Engaging your voice, speaking and being heard is transformational. It's powerful to use your throat to express these four words/phrases: No! Stop! Back off! F*ck off! Often our boundaries were invaded as children. Directing these words towards traits we are done with is a way of setting a boundary around unconsciously replaying that trait. A good contained place to 'voice' is driving in your car by yourself, ideally on a quiet country road. Turn up the music and scream! Shout into a pillow if the neighbours are about. Use your tennis racquet or similar to hit a mattress – and scream. Making sounds is profoundly healing, particularly if you grew up with the Victorian rule that children are to be 'seen and not heard'. You can also engage a singing or voice coach to help you open up your voice.

RE-MOTHERING

Acknowledgement, praise and validation may have been lacking in your family. Or perhaps your parents, in their enthusiasm to build the esteem they lacked, overdid it. It's time to pat yourself on the back and tell yourself well done for completing the Deep Dives and activities around the Tricky Traits you took on from your mother.

You are ready to take on the job of re-mothering yourself. This means giving yourself all that you wanted from your mother that she wasn't able to give. Re-mothering, learning to care, nurture, and delight in yourself all take practice. Here's a useful list of ways to re-mother your precious being (*Step 8* will give you more direction on this):

> You are ready to take on the job of re-mothering yourself

13 RE-MOTHERING RESETS

1. Celebrate yourself. Let yourself know and enjoy your own beauty and splendour.

2. Listen to how you feel, and trust your feelings.

3. Make self-care a priority.

4. Nourish your body well and move your body in Joyful ways.

5. Find gentle ways to connect and flow with your body, like yin yoga, dance, swimming and walking.

6. Respect your need for growth and evolution.

7. Support, validate and encourage yourself.

8. Become boundary savvy.

9. Find mentor-mothers, women who are older or wiser than you who offer sage insight and point out fresh paths.

10. Create and join support networks with other women you can count on.

11. Make regular time and space to chill out, recover and regenerate.

12. Spend time with Mother Nature.

13. Practise delighting in all of life, including the difficult and messy stuff.

> "You yourself, as much as anybody in the entire universe, deserves your love and affection."
>
> GAUTAMA BUDDHA

TLDR TOO LONG DIDN'T READ

- Ⓙ Your mother's attitudes, thoughts, feelings and ways of being in a relationship had a profound impact on shaping you.

- Ⓙ You took in her thoughts, feelings, rules, praise and punishment directly as she interacted with you.

- Ⓙ You also took her in by witnessing how she interacted with your dad/her partner, the family, work and the world.

- Ⓙ As an adult, your job is to celebrate the wonderful parts you absorbed from her and challenge the parts you learnt from her that no longer serve you.

- Ⓙ You got enough – you are alive and breathing today. Give yourself permission to take care of the rest.

- Ⓙ What Tricky Traits no longer serve you? Use the Deep Dives, themes and raw feelings letter to explore and name the traits.

- Ⓙ As you name the difficult traits, your awareness may be enough to create a shift.

Ⓙ︎ⓁYou can use dance, movement, shaking, breathwork, painting and voicing to move 'Sticky' Tricky Traits and create more space to connect with your delight.

Ⓙ︎ⓁExplore what you needed from Mum as a child and teenager but didn't receive, and give those permissions, experiences, validation and things directly to yourself. This is re-parenting, where you take responsibility for your delight and self-nurturance.

STEP 3

RECOGNISE THE IMPACT: YOUR FATHER

"Listen to the father,
who is within you."

JASON SHULMAN

You have made a phenomenal effort identifying, naming and transforming the Tricky Traits you inherited from Mum. Now you will explore the influence of Dad (or your male caregiver) and the traits you adopted from him.

Your father exploration needs to include any significant person in your childhood who took on the male caretaker role or surrogate father role. This includes stepfathers, elder brothers, uncles, grandfathers or boarding school masters who took on the role of fathering you.

As you read the questions, which are designed to help you identify the imprints from your father or surrogate dad, be awake to your feelings, sensations and thoughts. Listen to the loud *ahas* as well as the whispers.

THE ROLE OF THE FATHER

As you read the themes and questions and identify a trait, ask yourself in relation to Dad:

1. How was it as a child? Which Tricky Traits did I learn from Dad directly or via trauma I experienced involving him?

2. How is it now, acting out this trait?

3. What is the negative impact of this particular trait on my life?

4. Do I want to continue with this difficult pattern in my life or do I want to let it go?

FATHER THEMES

Your father's primary role was probably quite different from your mum's. And he is likely to be a very different character. Although you will engage in the same practice of 'Spot the Tricky Traits', the flavour with Dad will be different.

One of the major themes around Dad is how his absence, presence or engagement impacted you. Often fathers are away from their families working long hours or in another city or country. Or he may be physically present but emotionally unavailable. We name that Tricky Trait 'there but not there'. How was he with you as a child? What Tricky Traits did you learn from direct experience and his modelling around the themes below?

> One of the major themes around Dad is how his absence, presence or engagement impacted you

* Relationships
* Self-worth
* The outside world: adventure
* Work/career
* Money
* Authority
* Enforcing rules and boundaries
* Spiritual connection
* Gender

Deep Dive
TRICKY TRAITS FROM DAD

Journal your responses to these questions, listing any Tricky Traits you become aware of. Before you explore this Deep Dive into the traits you learnt from Dad, remind yourself of the three inner steps: *Awareness, Owning, Action.*

Take a few breaths. Allow your attention to move into your body. Get comfortable. As you sit, with your journal or writing device ready, feel the support of the cushions under you and behind you. Relax your shoulders. Soften any areas of tension. You are safe, and it's safe to know your own reality.

Gently take your imagination and awareness all the way back to the time of your conception. The questions will then lead you through stages of your life:

* Was your dad physically present at your birth?
* Do you know what was going on with your father when your mother was pregnant with you? Were things in a settled place?
* How do you think he felt about your arrival?
* Did he play with you when you were small?
* Did he include you in his activities and interests?
* Did he spend time with you, talking and listening, nurturing your interests? Or was he busy working or involved in community activities? How available was he?
* Were you precious to him?

* Do you feel valued in your closest relationships? Do you value yourself?
* What impact has his presence or absence had on how you show up in your current relationships?
* Did he love and celebrate your mother? Did he support your mother emotionally?
* How do you support yourself emotionally? Are you able to host and welcome all your feelings?
* If you are a woman, consider what you learnt from Dad in terms of how you relate to men. How do you relate to men as friends, lovers or partners?
* If you're a man, what have you taken from Dad about what it means to be a man? How do you connect to other men? How do you relate to women as friends, lovers or partners?
* How did Dad relate to the parts of himself we often deem feminine – nurture, care and vulnerability? Did he express his emotions?
* How did he relate to the parts of himself deemed masculine – aggression, competition and providing for/protecting his family?
* As a consequence of what he valued, how do you relate to these masculine and feminine aspects within yourself?
* Did your father take care of his body and health?
* How does this inform your care for your body and health?
* Was he emotionally and sexually faithful to your mother?
* How did he relate to your body as you went through puberty? Was he involved in your sex education, or was that left to your mother or avoided altogether?
* What traits did you take on from his modelling around sexuality?
* What were your father's attitudes to work? Did he love it or hate it? Was work more important than being with the family? How did he relate to the structures at work?

- What beliefs and attitudes have you taken from him around work?
- And money? Was your father paid well for the work he did? Was there enough money for your family's needs? Did he manage money well with savings and investments?
- What was his attitude towards money? Was he generous or mean with money?
- What are your beliefs about money? Does it flow freely? Does it feel like a struggle? Are you ever satisfied?
- What was your father's relationship to authority? Did he embrace structure and consistency? Was he fair and just at home? Or was he a tyrant?
- As a consequence, how are you with authority now – respectful, fearful or rebellious?
- If he used addictive substances or behaviours to numb himself, what impact did this have on you?
- How did your dad relate to his spirit, to his connectedness to life? Was he black-and-white in his spiritual beliefs? How did he relate to religion or spirituality?
- What is your relationship like with the spiritual world? Religion? Are you able to nurture your own spirit and explore your own spirituality?

TRICKY TRAIT CHECKLIST

Here's another list of traits to support you in your trait detection. It builds on the one we saw in *Step 2*. Check if you experienced any of this kind of hurt or trauma in relation to your father or father figures. Reflect on how it impacted you and how you may now do it to yourself or others. Look at how your father may have acted out these traits but also where he couldn't or didn't protect you from others.

STEP 3

Abandonment
Abuse of any kind
(physical, mental, emotional, sexual, sp...
Belittling
Betraying
Breaking promises
Bullying or overpowering
Competing
Controlling
Criticising
Cruelty
Deceiving
Disapproving
Discrediting
Disgracing
Dismissing
Humiliating
Ignoring
Inflicting fear
Inflicting guilt
Intimidating
Invalidating
Joking about or teasing
Laughing at
Limiting
Making vague demands
Manipulating
Misleading
Neglecting

Passive
Patronising
Responding inconsistently
Stifling
Withdrawing
Withholding love

CREATING EVEN MORE SPACE

In the letter-writing process outlined next, you'll have another opportunity to write your truth. You've already practised this tool with Mum. Again, writing out our feelings with the intention of releasing them helps us to create more space in our being. Out of this spaciousness we can make our own fresh choices.

Many of us came from families where the rule was to never express painful or difficult feelings. Our angry and hurt feelings went underground, along with our Joy. Often, we don't know how or what we feel until we write or speak our thoughts and feelings.

Allow yourself to access your heart, your vulnerability and your child within as you write. There may be many feelings not included in the list below. Please ad-lib and express your emotional truth. For example, the young part of you may resonate

> Often we don't know how or what we feel until we write or speak our thoughts and feelings

with some of these difficult feelings: you may feel hopeless, lost, frozen, stupid, terrified, overwhelmed, out of control, humiliated, shattered, lonely… the list of possible feelings is long. The Feelings List on my website (andreaanstiss.com/juicylife) may help you identify and name your feelings. These are feelings we may not have been able to name or express because we didn't have the language or we were not allowed to express them. Use the words that fit for you.

You may want to change the stem sentences to write in the past tense. For example, it may be easier to connect with your unacknowledged feelings if you write "I felt angry" or "I was angry" rather than "I feel angry". Using the past tense "I felt…" may support you to access the voice of that little child within. Experiment with the raw feelings letter and discover what works for you.

> It's safe to know what you know and validate your own truth

These letters (you may need to write several) will never be sent, so it's a safe and contained way to acknowledge and release difficult feelings.

RAW FEELINGS LETTER

You are now becoming expert at expressing yourself in this way. Let yourself go for it. Be radically honest. Your father or surrogate father will never read this. It's safe to know what you know and validate your own truth.

Dear Dad or significant father figure,

I am writing this letter to share my feelings with you:

For Anger

I don't like it
I feel frustrated
I am angry that
I am resentful that
I feel annoyed
I wanted
I want

For Sadness

I feel disappointed
I am sad that
I feel hurt that
I wanted
I want

For Fear

I feel worried
I am afraid
I feel scared
I am anxious that
I don't want
I need
I wanted
I want

For Regret

I feel embarrassed
I am sorry
I feel ashamed
I don't want
I wanted
I want

Anthony's story

Anthony came to see me soon after he broke off his engagement with his fiancée. For the past year his fiancée had been unemployed, and Anthony had been using his income to pay for food and rent for both of them. He was uncertain about their future together as he felt an unsettling combination of boredom, heaviness and terror about his future responsibilities as a provider, a partner and a father. He also felt unchallenged in his job but could see few opportunities for upgrading within his company or with any of the competitors. He wanted clarity about how he'd ended up in such an empty place at the age of thirty.

As we dived deeper into his history, Anthony told me that when he was 12 years old, his dad left his mum to look for work in a neighbouring country. Anthony remained with his mum and younger sister. He became the 'man' of the house and was also lassoed into the role of go-between, where he had to relay upsetting information from his father to his mother. Every month, he had to dole out his father's earnings to his father's brothers – leaving very little money for his mum, his sister and him to scrape by.

His father quickly found another woman and began divorce proceedings against Anthony's mum. His father was too cowardly to speak directly with his wife; Anthony had to mediate. He was burdened with information that should have remained the business of his parents. His mother was devastated by the divorce, and Anthony spent his teenage years caring for her emotionally: witnessing her tears, consoling her and attempting to carry some of her grief. To supplement the family income, he spent his after-school hours working. And although he connected with his uncles, he missed his father deeply.

He began the raw feelings letter-writing process with his former fiancée first. Knowing this was not a letter to be sent but an opportunity to discover hidden feelings and traits, Anthony dumped all his resentment onto the page. Encouraged by a sense of release from admitting his truth to himself, he moved on to his mother. He made it clear it wasn't his job to care for her emotionally and that he was not and never had been responsible for her happiness. That was her job. In the space of his father leaving and his parents' divorce, Anthony's boundaries had been lost. He clearly recognised the trait of over-caring, something he learnt because of the love he had for his mother and sister. He had repeated the Tricky Traits of over-caring and people-pleasing with his previous girlfriends and his fiancée. In his giving, he had given himself away.

Next, he wrote letters to his father, some of them in thick red ink reflective of his rage. He saw soon enough that his rage was protecting the deep fear and hurt of that twelve-year-old who had to take on far too much responsibility. These were his teen years – when he should have been hanging out with his friends and discovering life beyond his family roles. He took some weeks to grieve his lost teenage years, but all was not lost.

As Anthony made more space for what he wanted for his one precious life, he released the guilt about ending his relationship. He soon met a new girlfriend who was more independent both emotionally and financially. He set clear boundaries when she pushed to move in with him, and they continued their romance living in separate apartments. He plainly explained to her that now was his time and that he had some wild years to catch up on. He prioritised his need for adventure and with his male friends took the journeys he would have loved to have taken with his dad: climbing Mount Kilimanjaro and trekking in Nepal.

Emboldened by his fresh 'I've-got-this' attitude, he took the opportunity to speak in person with his father. Although Anthony was nervous about the meeting, he challenged himself to express his sadness and disappointment directly, as well as his love for his dad. It wasn't easy but it was radically freeing. He realised, despite all the hurt and resentment he had towards his dad, that there was a love that had never left. In resolving the pain he held towards his father, the biggest authority figure in his life, Anthony then felt confident to speak directly to his boss, regardless of the outcome. His boss agreed to offer him more rewarding projects. Anthony made it clear that if these were not forthcoming, he would leave in six months.

STICKY TRICKY TRAITS – EMBODIED LETTING GO

In *Step 2* we looked at six creative ways of 'embodied letting go' – releasing outdated traits and creating more spaciousness in your being. I encourage you to reread those suggestions and consider what will support you with the traits you adopted from your father. There are some extra 'letting go' tools below. If they resonate, use them as additional ways to release any Tricky Traits – regardless of who you learnt them from.

My friend Samar Ajami, a Nondual Healing teacher, describes her experience of 'embodied letting go' as more an experience of acceptance: "A relaxed stance of letting everything into my being, exactly as it is – this gives rise to a vivid sensation in my body of a flowing river – with so much aliveness." Explore your own ways of letting go.

Embodied letting go – four additional experiences

1. *The boxing bag*
   Identify the traits you need to release. Write them on a small piece of paper. Show up at your local boxing class or get hold of a boxing bag. Put the folded paper inside your boxing glove and begin punching with the intention of letting go. Let yourself punch until the sweat is running down your back, or at least until you feel a sense of liberation. Let's be clear, you are not punching your father, you are creating fresh space in your being. And if you had a violent parent, this may be a really liberating method of trait release. However, you will want to go slowly. You may also want to explore this method with a therapist or someone trained in trauma-release work so you feel fully supported and safe.

2. *The long run*
   The long run is similar to boxing but the focus is more on your feet. Put the Tricky Traits, written on a small card, between your laces and the tongue of your running shoes. Or, using indelible ink, write the traits on the soles of your shoes. Run hard. Run long. Pound those old traits into the path. Use your breath to take in renewed space and freedom.

3. *Endless athleticism!*
   You can morph this method for any sporting activity, from

swimming to darts. I'm an avid tennis player. The act of hitting a ball really hard is enormously helpful for releasing difficult feelings, especially the Tricky Traits of anger and frustration.

4. *'Sitting with'*

The 'sitting with' method of trait release is about creating space by staying with a Sticky Tricky Trait and feeling the energy of this trait vividly. It's a method that has its roots in meditation practice, where we practise staying with our difficulties and our painful feelings rather than fleeing from them. As we sit and feel into the shape and flavour of a particular Tricky Trait with intensity, what happens surprisingly often is that the heaviness of the trait begins to dissolve. Fresh energy begins to move through our body.

Long-time meditators explain that by giving space to difficult traits in this way, the energy they are made of dissolves and returns to the source from which all of life comes. It's as if we are returning fragments that have been split from the whole and want to return to the whole. This meditative release might appeal if you want a gentler approach or if you are unable to engage physically in the other ways I've described.

RE-FATHERING

Re-parenting – giving yourself all that you wanted from your parents that they weren't able to give – is an art that you already have some understanding of around re-mothering. Re-fathering has a different invitation and intention from re-mothering. Only you know what you missed out on or what was overdone by Dad. Trust that inner knowing. Here are some ideas for developing a loving inner father:

TEN RE-FATHERING RESETS

1. Take action; back up your feelings with action.

2. Create structure and boundaries and uphold them.

3. Get comfortable with money, prosperity and wealth.

4. Make friends with time management.

5. Feel your deepest passion and follow that thread.

6. Take risks.

7. Let yourself experience healthy emptiness.

8. Be generous to yourself.

9. Embrace excellence.

10. Love leadership.

> "Envisioning our father's suffering allows us to gain a new perspective on who he is as a whole person and how he adopted his own patterns."
>
> ERICA GARZA

TLDR   TOO LONG DIDN'T READ

- Ⓙ Your father's behaviours, attitudes, thoughts, feelings and ways of being had a profound impact on shaping you.

- Ⓙ You took in his thoughts, feelings, rules, praise and punishment directly as he interacted with you.

- Ⓙ You also took in his strengths and weaknesses by witnessing how he interacted with your mother, the extended family, work and the world.

- Ⓙ The relationship you witnessed between your mother and father has created much of your blueprint for how you relate to your beloved/partner.

- Ⓙ Give yourself permission to take action and take care of the places where you may have felt, for example, unseen, criticised, neglected or abandoned by Dad.

- Ⓙ What Tricky Traits adopted from your father no longer serve you? Use the Deep Dives, themes and raw feelings letter to explore and name the traits.

- Ⓙ As you name the difficult traits, your awareness may be enough to create a shift.

- Ⓙ You can use a variety of 'embodied letting go' experiences to move and integrate Sticky Tricky Traits and create more space to connect with your True Self and Juicy presence.

- Ⓙ Explore what you needed as a child from your dad and didn't receive, and give those permissions, validation, celebration and material things directly to yourself. This is re-parenting, where you step up and take responsibility for your fulfilment and Joy.

STEP 4

RECOGNISE THE IMPACT: YOUR ANCESTORS

*"You are the dream of
all your ancestors."*

BERT HELLINGER

In the first few Steps we explored the Tricky Traits we adopted from our parents and how these traits impacted us as individuals. Now we move deeper into naming the big events and sweeping patterns of our ancestors. It's likely that some of these larger influences, which impact you as an individual and each family member, are fuelling some of your more hidden traits. This work will help you shine the light of awareness on your deep Trances that feel murky or frightening – the patterns you may wish to deny or numb out.

Many of us take on damaging patterns such as depression, anxiety and guilt as a way of 'belonging' in our families. For example, a child may sacrifice their own Joy in a vain attempt to ease the pain of another family member, often a parent. Being aware of this helps us to see clearly what we may be 'carrying' for another family member and the cost to us. Then we can let go and access our own True Self as we move forward.

In exploring the larger movements of our ancestors, we more easily develop compassion and respect for our parents. We will have more understanding of why our parents were the way they were. We can open our hearts to them and their suffering, without absorbing their pain. By envisioning our parents' difficulties and respecting their paths, we learn we no longer need to carry their burdens.

INVISIBLE TIES THAT BIND

I invite you to be open to an adventure, to come with me on a magical mystery tour where you will explore the power of your lineage using 'Family Constellations'. This work feels magical because we are exploring the *invisible* ties that bind us as we discover we are a part of an enormous unseen energy field that spans generations. Family

Constellation work powerfully restores not just our own connection to our True Selves but also the peace and emotional freedom of generations to come.

Family Constellations help to disclose the deeper forces that unknowingly influence our thoughts, behaviours and emotional experiences through multiple generations. Using this modality, we are less focused on how we feel about certain family members – 'Mum is pushy' or 'Dad is unavailable', for example – and instead we look at the events and the known facts of the family, such as the early death of parents and grandparents, the death of an infant or someone young, adoptions or the exclusion of someone.

Entanglements

Most of the events we consider in Family Constellations may have occurred long before we were born. Sometimes these events or people have an 'unspeakability' or shame attached to them, and so are swept under the carpet. But down the family line there is a child who is carrying the feelings of that person and the pain of that burden, even though they have never met that relative. In Constellations speak, these are called 'trans-generational entanglements'.

As we do this powerful repair work detangling the tangles, we open ourselves to deep respect for our ancestors and fresh insights into our family dynamics. This broader lens of the whole family system gives us understanding, the ability to come to terms with long-held grief, and true appreciation of the value of our lives. Knowing the value of our lives nourishes our urgency to connect with our True Selves and live with intensity. This has a positive healing impact on all parts of our being – body, mind and spirit. Doing Family Constellations work clears the way for the next generation to be free of these hidden patterns and burdens. It creates more spaciousness and Joy for your descendants – and for the world!

I have experienced a profound sense of wholeness and peace from participating in this seemingly magical modality. And I have been privileged to witness participants in multiple Family Constellations groups experience an enormous sense of relief as flow, order and balance are restored.

> **Doing Family Constellations work clears the way for the next generation to be free of these hidden patterns and burdens**

YOUR ROOTS

> "A wave is born from deep conditions of the ocean.
> A person is born from deep conditions of the world."
>
> RUTH OZEKI

We are born from deep conditions of the world, and the first condition of the world is that we are born into an already existing family system. This is a system that stretches across generations and across time. I invite you to explore and uncover hidden loyalties, life events and family history that have been buried in time.

Difficult fates

Let's start with a list of greater forces or events that may have occurred in a family system and that will leave a powerful imprint, referred to in Constellations as 'difficult fates':

* Early death of parents or grandparents
* Death of an infant or someone young
* Accidental deaths and murders
* Abortions, terminations, miscarriages and stillbirths
* Divorces
* Previous significant relationships, such as a former spouse or first love
* Extramarital births (in the past and where it caused social disturbance)
* Adoptions
* Anyone who has been forced into the role of black sheep or is considered to be the black sheep of the family
* Ill-gotten wealth
* Bankruptcies and other economic losses
* Suicide
* Family members sent at a young age to boarding school without necessary reason
* Family members never allowed to leave the parental home
* Nuns, monks or priests in the family
* Greater forces such as wars, genocides, colonisation, famine, natural disasters, pandemics, migration and immigration

Later we will explore and name the difficult fates that specifically impacted you and your family.

EVERYONE BELONGS

We are bound to our family system by a deep need to belong.

A child will do anything for the love of a parent. That is why we absorb their destructive Tricky Traits. The bond to our parents and to our families begins even before birth; we belong to families that go back generations.

When your grandmother was pregnant with your mother, she carried part of you too. Your mother was born with the eggs that created you.

Belonging and connections are a source of power when the energy within the family system is clear and love flows. But when there is a blockage in the flow, an entanglement, the family and each person in the system is potentially weakened.

> We are bound to our family system by a deep need to belong

FAMILY CONSTELLATIONS GROUP WORK

Family Constellations are usually facilitated in person (in groups or one-to-one) or online. However, as you engage in the Constellation Deep Dives and experiences offered in this Step, you too will sense powerful shifts in your awareness. Once you have had a flavour of the power of Family Constellations, you may choose to experience group work.

In a group constellation, a client chooses individuals from the attendees, who are often unknown to her, to represent her family members. This includes someone to represent the client themselves. With minimal explanation, the client positions these people to stand in for original family members. The representatives are placed, without any gestures, in any way the client feels is in some kind of constellation.

As Family Constellations expert Svagito Liebermeister explains in *The Zen Way of Counseling*, what is created is "a portrait of the client's family: a configuration that expresses something about the degree of intimacy, pain, love, or sense of abandonment that each family member feels in relation to the others".

The representatives take on the feeling and behaviour of the people they are representing. With the support of a Constellations therapist, the stand-ins change position as the session unfolds. They are then given short sentences to say, usually simple one-liners. These sentences contain deep truths about the relationships between the family members they are representing. As the work progresses, the representatives find different positions in relation to each other where everyone feels more at ease. The client remains an observer for much of the session, but towards the end they may join the constellation, taking their place within the family.

The Constellations modality is helpful for finding your place within the family system and for leaving the suffering with your parents or your grandparents. This allows you to look at each of them with greater understanding and compassion. It means you can sincerely thank your parents and ancestors for your life – with the profound understanding that without them, you would not be here. You may arrive at an embodied sense of 'Thank you, Mum and Dad, I received enough'. This is a powerful outcome and frees you to move out into life as a grown-up.

A MYSTERIOUS FIELD

Behind the dynamics of Family Constellations is an invisible field of energy. This field is sometimes called the Knowing Field or, according to Rupert Sheldrake, the Morphic Field. Connecting with this mysterious field of energy, participants are able to access feelings and perceptions of the client's family members they represent. Usually, the participants in the groups have never met before or know very little about each other. This is where the mystery opens up! It's a magical and uncanny feeling to step into a family's energy field and instantly perceive certain truths about the relationships within that system.

This work can lift the veil of our cultural amnesia, a thick denial that often leaves us feeling isolated and numb. We often live in separation from our families. Constellations show us plainly that we are all interconnected – we are all a part of this precious web of life. This work leads us back into unity, not only with ourselves but also with the family systems into which we were born. It is a deep 'yes' to life and to everything that happened before us. This, in turn, gives us permission to say 'yes' to ourselves.

HEALING SENTENCES

Healing sentences in Constellation work are considered the language of the soul. They are designed to move us out of story and opinion to simply stating what is. They are spoken with reverence, and my experience is that the right statement reverberates powerfully across time and space. Healing sentences restore, honour our history and bring us into connection. Our soul is always longing for simple words. Below are some simple healing sentences that have been used to create a healing movement for clients and their family systems. I invite you to try the one(s) that are relevant to your journey.

Close your eyes and imagine yourself standing in front of the family member I refer to. Pay attention to how close you are standing to the person in front of you – or how far away you are – before saying the healing sentence. You may also use a photograph of the person. Repeat the sentence several times and notice what feelings come up for you.

> Healing sentences restore, honour our history and bring us into connection

Child to mother: *"I now take you as my mother."*

Child to father: *"You did what you could. Thank you."*

Early death of a sibling: *"You have a special place in my heart."*

In the case of divorce, to your former partner: *"When I look at our children and I see a part of you in them, I love that about them."*

To a partner: *"Here, you are just my partner."* (This expression honours that a partner is not a parent and that a partner does not have this level of influence.)

Child to grandmother: *"Without you I wouldn't be here."*

PRINCIPLES FOR RESTORING LOVE

In a Family Constellation, the underlying principles are the guiding force – whether you are working in a group or on your own. Hold these principles close as you respond to the Deep Dive questions about your family system later in the chapter.

Three principles for restoring love in the family system

1. *Belonging*

    Who belongs (in this family)? Who is excluded? (This refers to family members who have been forgotten, condemned or rejected because they may have somehow brought shame to the family.)

2. *Order*

    Who comes first? In the sibling birth order, those born earlier have a certain priority over those who were born later. The order of parents/partners also applies. For example, the first wife will always be the first wife, whether in a culture of multiple wives (such as in the Middle East) or after divorce. She belongs in that position and deserves that respect from the second wife and wider family.

3. *Balance*

    Is there a balance between giving and taking? This refers to the giving of parents to the child and the taking of the child from the parents and not the other way around. Often children have a sense of their parent's pain or helplessness and attempt to carry their parent's pain out of love for that parent, at enormous cost to their own happiness. Parents will always give more. Any other relationship beyond the parent-child relationship can only last with an equal balance of giving and taking.

SIBLING STRIFE

Our relationship with a sister or brother may be filled with warmth, support and connection. Or it could feel like a bloody battleground. The bond with our siblings is profound and enduring, even if we're not on talking terms or if our siblings passed away decades ago.

Siblings share either both or one of the same parents. When we have challenges with our friends, peers or colleagues, this is a sign we need to explore the often hidden dynamics at play with our siblings. They were our first friends and provided the blueprint for our peer relationships.

From a Family Constellations perspective, the root cause of sibling issues is related to unconscious dynamics and loyalties and the importance of honouring each sibling's place in the line. We may have a loyalty to one parent while our sibling is loyal to another parent. This will impact our relationship with that sibling.

Seven keys to help sibling skirmishes

Let me offer seven 'keys' to help to increase your awareness about the roots of sibling conflict. If you have sibling issues and want to unearth what may be happening, take your pen and paper or writing device and journal what resonates or rattles within you.

1. *Honour* the siblings that came first. The firstborn often carries more responsibility than the secondborn.

2. *Take* your right place in the sibling line. This means including siblings who were terminated, miscarried and stillborn. We also need to include siblings from any other relationships our parents may have had. In the Gulf countries, where many of my clients come from, the father has multiple wives, so there is some complexity to ensuring inclusiveness and taking your right place in the sibling line.

3. *Give* everyone else their place according to their order of arrival in the family. We need to be wary of acting like the surrogate parent of our siblings or the child of our siblings.

4. *Avoid* comparing yourself to your siblings, and challenge the comparisons that parents may have projected onto you.

5. *Respect* the special relationship your parents had with each one of your siblings. It's helpful to remember that being too close to a parent or being a 'favourite' or 'golden child' can be more of a burden than a blessing.

6. *Recognise* that the sibling labelled the black sheep is usually carrying more trauma for the family than the other siblings.

7. *Be aware* that conflict between father and mother can often transmit a conflict between siblings by one sibling sympathising with one parent and another sibling taking the side of the other parent.

DEEP DIVE
YOUR FAMILY SYSTEM

I invite you to increase your awareness about your own family system and the entanglements within it by responding to some key questions. Use your felt-sense – the sensations in your body – to guide you in your responses.

These questions are sometimes given to clients preparing to do a Family Constellation. In simply responding honestly to these questions, you will connect with a deeper strength and compassion. And as you explore this and every Deep Dive, remember the three inner steps from earlier: *Awareness*, *Owning* and *Action*.

Right now, the task is to become super curious about your family system. Allow yourself to be comfortable. Have your pen and journal or writing device next to you. Take a few breaths. Allow your attention to move into your body. As you sit, feel the support of the cushions under you and behind you. Relax your shoulders. Soften any areas of tension. You are safe, and it's safe to know your own reality. Remember to breathe deeply.

Facts from your childhood
* Were there complications with your birth?
* Was your mother ill, or did she have a permanent injury as a result of your birth?
* Were you hospitalised early or later on in childhood due to a serious illness?
* How many siblings do you have?
* Were there any miscarriages, or children who died at a young age?
* Did any of your siblings suffer a 'difficult fate' (check the list from earlier)?
* What is your heritage and who immigrated? Where were you born? Why did your family come to this country?

Facts from your adolescence/adulthood
* Were there important partners (first great loves) before your current couple relationship?
* Were there special reasons for the premature end to an earlier relationship, for example from parental influence?
* Were there any abortions?
* Were there any miscarriages, or children who died at a young age?
* Were there extramarital births?
* Were there children from an earlier relationship?

Facts from your parents
- * How did your parents meet?
- * Did one of them have an important couple relationship previously or was he or she married before? What happened in that relationship?
- * How old were they when they married?
- * Were you born before or after they married?
- * Were you the reason they married?
- * If they didn't marry, was there a special reason for this?

Facts from your mother's/father's family of origin
- * How many siblings did he or she have, and where in the order did he or she come in the family?
- * Were there any miscarriages, abortions or children who died at a young age?
- * Was there a difficult fate (refer to the list of difficult fates from earlier)?

Facts from each grandparent's family of origin
- * How many siblings did he or she have, and what was his or her position in the family?
- * Were there any miscarriages, abortions or children who died at a young age?
- * As a child or adult, did he or she undergo a difficult fate?

Great-grandparents and ancestors on both sides
- * Were there any difficult fates or notable events?

> "If you don't know history, then you don't know anything. You are a leaf that doesn't know it is part of a tree."
>
> **MICHAEL CRICHTON**

THE FAMILY TREE

Using the information you have gathered from the questions about your family system, I now invite you to complete your family tree. This experience will help you to see clearly some of the hidden patterns that are influencing you today. You will come to understand that many of your Tricky Traits didn't start with you – but they can end with you. This is a powerful way to make the unconscious patterns of the family conscious.

You may find it useful to download a template to help you map out your family tree (see https://freefamilytreetemplates.com for some examples). When you are ready to begin, gather the information you have about your family system and use the following notes to guide you:

Acknowledging absence

Marine Sélénée, *goop* contributor and author of *Connected Fates, Separate Destinies*, is a Family Constellations facilitator based in New York. She offers some creative ways of working with your tree:

> *"If you can't fill in all the branches of your family tree, start with the information you have. If you're dealing with the absence of a family member – like a parent or grandparent you never knew – that, too, can be represented by footprints. When you're looking at the footprint symbol on your tree, you could say something like 'I don't know what happened because I do not know your story. But what I know right now is that I have been suffering from it, and I want to acknowledge it'."*

Tree leaf details

As you draw your family tree, note the dates and events that feel important. Such as:

* Dates of birth
* Dates of death
* Graduations
* Marriages
* Divorces
* Abuse
* Depression/anxiety
* Career changes
* People ignored or not included for some reason
* Emigration

Spot the clues

Look for the patterns or repetition. You may notice shared birthdays or death anniversaries or even repeating illnesses. Perhaps there is a lineage of alcoholism or another form of addiction that you can detect moving through each generation. Perhaps traumatic events occurred at similar ages, or relatives were excluded from the family for some reason. You may become aware of details such as how your grandfather lost his property and money and how this took the family into a period of poverty. Or your grandmother had to flee her country during a revolution, which meant your father began his life on a new continent as a refugee. You might become aware that generations of women in your family suffered from depression. All of this may give you clues about your family and yourself.

As you look at the dates and events, notice the one that strikes you the most. Notice the event that gives you the most strength.

Sit, reflect and say thank you

Look at your family tree with love. Thank each member one by one for being part of your family.

How do you feel? Do you sense how you are part of a bigger picture?

Amy's story

Amy volunteered to do a Family Constellation in an evening session of Constellations offered monthly in our community. She rose enthusiastically from the floor cushion to take her seat at the front of the room next to our facilitator, MayBritt. Amy lifted her head to address the room; her dark, thick hair fell in waves over her shoulders. Her eyes lit up as if she knew something fascinating was about to happen.

"I have an eating disorder and I want to understand what my relationship with food is really about," she said. She explained that she binged on carbohydrates mostly and although her eating was sometimes okay, she reverted back to her chaotic eating when something upset her. This relationship with carbohydrates impacted her weight and her health.

MayBritt asked her about her first memories of her disturbed relationship with food. Amy explained that this was a challenge that had been with her for as long as she could remember. She had a clear memory of hiding inside a wardrobe as a three-year-old, with a handful of cookies she had grabbed from the kitchen cupboard.

MayBritt invited Amy to look around the room and choose two representatives: one person to represent her and another to represent the eating disorder.

Amy asked if I would stand in as the representative for her. I was honoured because this work requires so much trust. She chose another woman to represent her eating disorder and then arranged the two of us in the centre of the room to create the shape of the relationship she sensed between herself and her eating disorder. She stepped to the side to observe what would unfold. We, the representatives – now held by the 'knowing field' – listened to and moved with our impulses.

Standing in for Amy, I felt compelled to walk to the far end of the room and around a corner, partially out of sight. My eyes and those of the eating disorder representative were fixed on the floor. In Constellations, this gaze indicates an un-mourned death in the family system.

"Who died early, either in your life or in your mother's or father's life?" MayBritt asked gently.

Amy paused for a moment. "My mother's mother died when my mum was nine months old giving birth to another baby."

MayBritt then chose a representative for Amy's grandmother. The grandmother representative took her place, lying on the floor. Immediately, the eating disorder went over to the grandmother and sat on the floor holding the grandmother's outstretched arm.

For MayBritt, it was clear that the eating disorder morphed into Amy's mother. "The eating disorder really belonged to your mother," she explained. "So, Amy, your mother could never be fully available to you as she was grieving this very early loss. It's likely that you have been using carbs to fill that space of a mother who couldn't be fully present for you because of this terrible loss when she was so young."

As all of this was unfolding, I remained in my crouched position for what felt like ages, feeling dissociated and only vaguely aware of the movements and voices at the other end of the room. Then I heard MayBritt announce that this part of the Constellation was done. I shook myself to release the energy of Amy I had been carrying and sat down on the side to observe. (Because the 'energetic field' took over my awareness, I later required a debrief with MayBritt to understand what had happened in the first part of the Constellation.)

MayBritt explained again to the whole group, including Amy, "The way the eating disorder was pulled to the grandmother who had passed away shows us that the eating disorder belongs more to the mother than Amy. So, Amy, your mother could never be fully available to you as she was grieving this very early loss."

She invited Amy to take her own place in the Constellation and stand opposite her mother representative. Behind her mother, MayBritt placed a line of people to represent the maternal lineage of Amy's grandmothers. Her grandmother held the shoulder of her mother and behind her stood the great-grandmother holding the grandmother's shoulder. And at the back stood the great-great-grandmother representative.

As Amy took her own place in the Constellation, more important information was revealed: Amy's tendency is to go too close to her mother. This is a classic Sticky Tricky Trait of wanting to 'save and rescue' Mother. MayBritt invited Amy to take a few steps back, and everyone in the room felt a collective outbreath as Amy gave herself and her mother more space. With more space, Amy could now see and appreciate how her mother was leaning back into all the other mothers behind her. Amy, for the first time, could see her mother in her strength, rather than someone who needed rescuing.

MayBritt invited Amy to repeat the healing sentence 'I take you as my mother'. Amy repeated the sentence several times, each time her voice growing stronger and her compassion growing wider for herself and for the women in her family.

The mother lineage of power, love and beauty palpably stretched back into history, amplified by the full moon that was hanging beyond the window. The strength of these grandmother figures supporting her mother filled Amy's heart and the hearts of the observers at the same time. I, for one, had a grandmother who died young and whose absence deeply impacted my mother and me. The issues around 'Mother' are so primal they touch all of us.

When I met Amy a few months later, she told me that carbohydrates were no longer her habitual 'go-to'. She had employed a personal trainer and was enjoying the challenge of the gym and the energy she now had.

CALLING IN YOUR ANCESTORS – A MEDITATION

Having connected with your ancestors in the family tree experience, I now invite you to connect with the power of your ancestors in a beautiful meditation. This meditation was given to me by my dear friend MayBritt Searty, the Family Constellations facilitator in the case study above. The purpose of this meditation is to honour our ancestors and receive their blessings. By including everyone, you will walk forward into life more supported, more grounded and with an expanded heart.

I invite you to place your feet on the ground and close your eyes. Now become aware of the soles of your feet on the ground. Notice a certain vibration or sensation underneath the soles of your feet on the ground. Allow this sensation to move up through your entire body and allow it to settle in your heart.

Imagine yourself standing in front of your family of origin: your father and mother, your grandparents on both sides of your parents, uncles and aunts, great-grandparents, great-uncles and aunts, your sisters or brothers and anyone else who made life possible for you. You may include any significant prior partners of either of your parents.

You invite them to sit in a circle around you. You are standing in the middle of this circle. You look at each of them – you smile at each of them and they smile back at you. You might see someone you didn't know existed. Just know everyone is welcome and has the right to belong equally. They have all gathered around you to honour you and one another. Take some time in the middle of the circle receiving their blessings and their love. Feel how they are all welcoming you.

Now that you have taken every person into your heart, you will receive a creative sentence or a creative word. This is a sentence or word that will heal everyone at once. It is a sentence or word that will change everything for everyone, including you, at the same time. The sentence or word is being given to you now. Without putting words in your mouth, it might be as simple as 'Thank you', or 'You did enough', or 'Without you, I wouldn't be here'.

You share it with everyone and see their faces change and everyone relax.

You now place the sentence or word in your heart as you take a deep breath.

As you breathe out, your ancestors disappear. Just as your ancestors appeared in front of you, they all go again. You are now standing on your own – so please turn around. You stand face to face with your life. You share your healing words or sentence with life and notice how life is responding to your sharing. You tell life: "Thank you. I have come. I have arrived."

> "To suffer is a lot easier than change.
> In order to be happy one needs to have courage."
>
> **BERT HELLINGER**

TLDR TOO LONG DIDN'T READ

- (JL) You are part of a mysterious field of interconnectedness that includes your ancestors, sweeping world events and 'difficult fates'.

- (JL) Understanding your roots ultimately brings energy and Joy as family secrets, and difficult fates are acknowledged.

- (JL) Exploring our Family Constellation reveals the deeper and often hidden forces at play that influence us and our families across generations.

- (JL) In Family Constellations we look at and acknowledge the events and the known facts of the family, such as the early death of parents and grandparents.

- (JL) We are bound to our family system by a deep need to belong. A child will do anything for the love of a parent, including 'carrying' their parent's pain.

- (JL) Seeing ourselves through the broader lens of the whole family system gives us understanding, permission to accept ancient grief and true appreciation of the value of our life.

- (JL) In honouring our ancestors we move towards respect and compassion for our parents and ourselves. In doing this work we help to heal both our ancestors and our descendants.

- (JL) Everyone belongs. Family members who have been 'forgotten', condemned or rejected impact us and need to be included.

- Ⓙ Belonging, order and balance are essential for restoring love in our families and in our own hearts.

- Ⓙ Balance refers to the importance of the flow of 'love and giving' moving from adult to child – and not the other way around, where the child attempts to look after the parent.

- Ⓙ Healing sentences are particularly powerful words spoken with reverence. They honour what is and they transform our relationships across time and space.

- Ⓙ Belonging and connections are a source of power when the energy within the family system is clear and love flows. In this flow we can more easily be attuned to our True Selves.

STEP 5

IDENTIFY AND EMBRACE THE TRAUMA

---

*"Trauma sucks.
You don't."*

CHRISTINE CISSY WHITE

To some degree or another, almost all of us have experienced trauma. It seems to be part of the human condition, of living in this soft, vulnerable body. Healing our trauma is not just for ourselves; it's an intention that will make our whole world a lighter place.

So what exactly is trauma? Essentially, it is the response to a distressing or disturbing event that overwhelms our ability to cope. It often causes feelings of helplessness, unworthiness and shame that affect our ability to feel a full range of emotions and experiences. When we are hijacked by trauma symptoms, it's difficult to fully connect to our deep Joy and Juiciness.

In this Step we will dive into the impact of trauma and look at how to release ourselves from its grip. I'll support you to restore your mind-body connection, which, in turn, will support you to live from the fullness of your True Self.

EMBRACE YOUR TRAUMA

In order to heal your trauma, I invite you to lean into and embrace your trauma symptoms and the suffering that goes with them. Yes, it's a big ask and perhaps an uncomfortable request. Start by noticing the amount of time you may have wasted criticising, judging or avoiding 'feeling what you feel'. Often when we have been traumatised, we attempt to avoid and distract ourselves from the feelings that go with trauma rather than face them directly.

Fortunately, trauma healing is a topic that is commanding much attention in the healing and transformation community right now. Thanks to the dedication and research of luminaries such as Bessel van der Kolk, Peter Levine and Stephen Porges, we now have much more awareness about the impact of trauma, how widespread it is and effective ways to work with it.

The movers and shakers in this field

We know from the work of Bessel van der Kolk, a psychiatrist and researcher probably best known for his book *The Body Keeps the Score*, that trauma is not just about having really bad memories. His work demonstrates that the traumatised person's whole mind, brain and sense of self is changed in response to the trauma, which, in turn, affects their ability to be present in the here and now. While talking about trauma can be helpful to a degree, it doesn't go deep enough into the animal brain. Traumatic stress comes from this unconscious part of the brain and affects the whole being, putting the body into an almost permanent state of survival response activation. This understanding validates body-based (or somatic) therapies, such as Dr Peter Levine's 'Somatic Experiencing'. The reason Stephen Porges' work has also become so important, particularly his 'polyvagal theory', is because of his finding that trauma interferes with face-to-face communication. His work has helped to clarify where in the brain trauma makes it difficult to connect with other people and the need to learn very specific ways to activate the social engagement system.

> Trauma affects our ability to be present in the here and now

Where trauma occurs

Trauma symptoms often occur in environments where the following kinds of circumstances are present:

* Loss of control
* Betrayal
* Abuse of power
* Helplessness
* Pain
* Confusion
* Loss (such as the death of, injury to, or divorce from our primary caregivers)

Trauma symptoms may be the result of experiences we endured in our family as children and teenagers, such as ongoing physical abuse in the form of getting hit or slapped, perhaps in the name of 'discipline'. (You may have already begun to explore how trauma has impacted you in the prior Steps.) Or the traumatic experiences may have come from something that occurred at school or in the community, such as being teased or bullied for being different in a way that you could not help (for having big ears or a physical disability, for example). Trauma, as we saw in *Step 4*, can form part of a Family Constellation, or family system, and be handed down from generation to generation. Some traumas, such as those resulting from war, can be experienced nationwide. Devastating events such as genocide and refugee camps can impact everyone who lived through them.

In the Middle East, I have had the privilege to meet many extraordinary and resilient people from Lebanon who grew up during the civil war from 1975 to 1990, as well as Iraqis and Kuwaitis who were impacted by the first Gulf War. Because of the terror, loss and ongoing uncertainty that they survived, their frozenness and anxiety are often palpable.

My father fought in World War II. At the tender age of 23, he went to the Solomon Islands to fight the Japanese. His father fought in World

War I in France. Neither my grandfather nor my father, nor nations of servicemen, had the opportunity to process their trauma and grief about the horrors they had experienced.

TRAUMA TRAITS

There are four main ways our body responds to traumatic events. They are:

1. Freeze
2. Fight
3. Flight
4. Fawn

These nervous system responses have a powerful impact on how we interface with the world after experiencing trauma. If you suspect you may be in a trauma response, gather your journal or note-taking app and reflect on the questions below. Be sure to breathe as you read these questions. Notice sensations in your body, flashes of memory and your emotional response to these questions. Be wary of self-blame habits where you may judge yourself as wrong for having your reactions. And remember the three inner steps from earlier: *Awareness, Owning, Action*.

You may recognise that you have a mix of Trauma Traits. Don't expect yourself to fit neatly into one category or another.

Deep Dive
TRAUMA

Four Deep Dives about trauma

Ask yourself the following questions about your trauma:

Freeze

You may be experiencing a freeze response if you answer yes to some – or all – of the following questions:

* Do you feel dissociated or out of touch with your feelings or events happening in your life?
* Are you spaced out or out of rhythm, not quite present?
* Do you sense that you hold back both your anger and your sadness?
* Do you avoid human contact and prefer to isolate?
* Do you feel detached from life?
* Do you struggle to make decisions?
* Are you a 'duvet diver' or a hibernator?
* Do you feel dead inside?

Fight

You may be experiencing a fight response if you answer yes to some – or all – of the following questions:

* Are you aggressive?
* Do you dominate and control others?
* Do you push for power and control?
* Do you demand perfectionism from others?
* Do you bully yourself and others?
* Are you overly critical?
* Do you explode and rage?
* Are you violent with yourself and others?

Flight

You may be experiencing a flight response if you answer yes to some – or all – of the following questions:

* Do you experience feelings of anxiety and panic?
* Do you use addictions such as alcohol, overeating or 'workaholism' to avoid your feelings?
* Do you have obsessive and/or compulsive behaviours such as handwashing or constant checking of locks?
* Are you always on the go?
* Are you an overachiever, constantly striving?
* Have you taken flight from your body and live mostly in your head?
* Are you overly analytical?
* Are you an expatriate, or do you choose to live a long way from the place where you grew up?

Fawn

You may be experiencing a fawn response if you answer yes to some – or all – of the following questions:

* Are you very concerned with looking right and fitting in?
* Are you a people-pleaser often forgoing your own preferences?
* Are you co-dependent?
* Do you defer to others in decision-making?
* Is it difficult for you to stand up for yourself?
* Do you avoid conflict?

NAMING ABUSE

Behind our trauma symptoms often lies a direct experience of abuse or witnessing other people being violated in some way. Our experience of abuse may be so overwhelming that we live in a mentally foggy, emotionally frozen or depressed state for years, until we are able to name the abuse that occurred and embark on the healing journey.

Sometimes it's difficult to name the abuse because of how our innate survival instinct as children works. In a nutshell, children don't want to believe that their beloved parents are abusive, and so they protect themselves from this painful truth with thick layers of denial. These layers can stay in place well into adulthood. It is also often challenging to confront trauma because of the shaming, secrets, grooming and lies that may have occurred. I've heard countless times in my therapy room: "Yes, but it was normal for my mother [and/or father] to beat me and my siblings," and "Screaming and hitting are part of our culture. It's how they showed they cared." This kind of reasoning protects us from taking our inner child's side and from entering into the grieving process of healing trauma.

Denial and a disconnect from our feelings enable us to survive difficult and even terrible events in our lives. In the previous Step we saw how a child will do almost anything for the love of a parent. That holds true even when a parent or family member is being abusive. Unconsciously, a child often takes the side of the perpetrator and falsely believes that they themselves must be to blame or are 'bad'. They cannot possibly believe the parent or the perpetrator is bad or wrong because they innately know they must rely on the parent or perpetrator for their survival needs. They may feel protective towards the person who abused them and they may have been offered gifts or favours to keep quiet.

A child might be especially confused if they experienced physical pleasure, arousal or emotional intimacy from sexual abuse. This confusion makes it difficult for a child to speak up. It's possible to push painful, confusing and frightening traumas into our depths without remembering them until years later. It's also common to replay traumas, so that you find yourself experiencing more of the same painful emotions and situations that engendered those emotions, over and over. The replay seems to happen until we wake up to our own power to heal and transform the layers of trauma.

Four types of abuse

Look at the descriptions of the four main types of abuse below. Did you experience any of these kinds of violation or neglect as a child or a teenager? As you read the descriptions, breathe deeply and listen to the feelings and sensations in your body. Go gently; we are entering territory that can feel dark and difficult.

1. *Emotional abuse*

    Emotional abuse includes abandonment, betrayal, neglect and ignoring you. It also includes verbal abuse: teasing, calling you names, racist remarks, and remarks about your size or shape, gender or sexual orientation. Emotional abuse is also where you are expected to do things that don't match your age or stage of development. A classic and pervasive type of emotional abuse is a parent or a relative constantly criticising or berating a child. Emotional abuse is conveying to a child they are worthless, unloved or inadequate. Bear in mind that where there has been physical, sexual or spiritual abuse, there will always also be emotional abuse since it is impossible for humans not to be affected emotionally by these other forms of abuse.

2. *Physical abuse*

    Physical abuse includes hitting, beating, kicking, spitting on you, or you witnessing this happening to others. It also includes the neglect aspect where your physical needs aren't cared for: where you aren't provided with enough food, clothing, space to rest or shelter. Being raised in a violent family or a violent country where your physical safety has been threatened is both physically and emotionally traumatising. Children brought up in an environment of physical abuse and violence often tolerate that kind of behaviour in their own relationships as adults because they didn't experience respect or safety as a child.

3. *Sexual abuse*

   Sexual abuse includes making children watch sexual activities, involving children in looking at or producing sexual images, penetrative sexual acts or forced masturbation/sexual stimulation. Sexual abuse includes obvious abuse, such as incest or rape, but also includes more subtle forms of abuse, such as disparaging comments about someone's body shape. It can be an uncle making lewd comments about his niece's changing body. It can simply be a look that feels invasive or violating. Encouraging children to behave in sexually inappropriate ways, such as provocative dancing or inappropriate touch, is also abusive.

4. *Spiritual abuse*

   Spiritual abuse includes all of the above abuse experiences because the impact of abuse creates a disconnection from our innate worthiness as human beings. Abuse brings about shame, where we feel worthless, defective, like 'a piece of shit', dirty or unlovable. Spiritual abuse also occurs when we are forced to undertake a particular form of spiritual practice. Or when we are persecuted for our religious beliefs. Or when we are manipulated by religious lies such as 'all homosexuals will go to hell' or 'you must tithe 20% of your income to remain a member of our church' or 'you must forgive those who harm you if you yourself want to be forgiven'. Lies such as these instil in us the idea that we have to work hard to earn God's love, that we are not intrinsically valuable. And that our feelings are irrelevant.

> "There is no timestamp on trauma. There isn't a formula that you can insert yourself into to get from horror to healed. Be patient. Take up space. Let your journey be the balm."
>
> DAWN SERRA

THE THREE Bs

While there isn't a formula that works for everyone around healing, the 'Three Bs' are basic keys for transforming trauma and abuse. They are: 'Believing' it happened, 'Breaking' the silence and 'Banishing' the blame. The fourth key is 'Ditching the Toxic Shame', which we will explore later in *Step 7*.

The Three Bs can help one heal from trauma in the following ways:

1. *Believing it happened*
   A trauma experience can be so overwhelming it's possible to question whether it really happened. Or we may choose to minimise it – telling ourselves it wasn't really that terrible. Denial can kick in because the abuse experience was so frightening it was simply too much to take in. This is especially true if you were a child when the abuse or trauma occurred as you may not have had the emotional capacity to deal with your fear or terror. Addictions are a widely used way of avoiding, dulling or distracting ourselves from the feelings, sensations and memories of painful experiences. We need to trust our inner knowing about what our experience was in order to face our truth.

2. *Breaking the silence*

   This basic key enables us to speak out beyond the silence and fear to trusted friends, family or therapists. This means moving beyond any internalised self-blame or shame that might stop us from telling the truth. Expressing our experience, telling our story to safe friends and fully feeling and expressing our feelings is vital. Breaking the silence takes courage, especially if the perpetrator was someone influential.

3. *Banishing the blame*

   This means challenging your inner self-talk, including all those lies a perpetrator may have used to groom you. Falsities such as 'You made me do this' or 'You deserve this' or 'You enjoy it too' may have been used by the perpetrator to manipulate the victim. Challenging the self-blame or self-hate, which is carried by the inner child, allows for accountability to be returned to the perpetrator. In turn, this allows for the victim to understand how brave and skilful they were to survive. There is a shift out of victimhood into knowing you are an incredible survivor, worthy of love and acceptance. You made it out alive!

REPAIR OR REPEAT?

You have a whole expanse of life before you and a life force pulsing in a symphony of rhythms through your being, even if you have experienced intense trauma. There is part of you that has always remained whole and complete, a part that was untouched by even the darkest trauma. Healing is a choice and a commitment to reconnect with that part. Will you choose it?

Without healing trauma, we are likely, via our unconscious, to continue to replay the trauma, which then strengthens the negative cycle of pain and perpetuates the trauma ad infinitum. We will, without being fully aware, allow and experience similar situations to those that caused our original trauma.

For example, if you were molested as a child and had no safe person to speak with who could help you see it wasn't your fault, that your body is sacred and you have a right to be respected, you are likely to be wide open to similar boundary invasions. I have heard multiple stories of childhood sexual abuse followed by teenage rape and then subsequent abusive adult relationships. Often there is also addiction, which is a symptom of the underlying pain. The addiction adds to the layers of shame and hopelessness, which, in turn, make adult intimate relationships desolate.

Remembering the original trauma we experienced as children, creating a loving relationship with that little inner child who survived and is still inside us, and grieving all they missed out on creates repair. Meeting your inner child with the love and understanding they are starved of releases you from the compulsion to repeat the pain over and over. It allows for the hurt part of you to be re-parented with love and understanding. If we choose to ignore our trauma, we inevitably pass it on, creating suffering for future generations.

You don't need to take the trauma-healing journey on your own. It's likely you have already experienced far too much isolation and loneliness. Please request the support you deserve. There are devoted and skilled trauma therapists and healers working in networks across the globe who can help you. Being mirrored and witnessed by a therapist you personally vibe with is a powerful way to transform. There are donation-based 12-step programmes, including CoDA (Co-Dependents Anonymous) and ACoA (Adult Children of Alcoholics), which provide structure and a safe space for you to undertake the Three Bs. When you are ready, you may also wish to join a healing group. There are healing groups and circles where leaders and participants provide support for fellow trauma survivors. The intention of these groups is to support members to move from surviving to thriving. With just an internet connection, you can connect to these resources from even the remotest location. You can remain a victim, or you can celebrate being a survivor and evolve into a human being who has an abundance of patience and compassion for self and others.

Sunita's story

Sunita, a stunningly beautiful young lawyer, connected with me for Zoom sessions to explore her boyfriend troubles. She was caught in a 'push-pull', 'come here, go away' relationship with a "boy" she'd been speaking with and occasionally meeting for two years. She didn't want the relationship but equally she couldn't let him go. She'd had a slew of previous boyfriends who had also disappointed her.

She wasted lots of time obsessing about why her latest guy hadn't contacted her and then why he suddenly did. She obsessed about her social media posts and why he looked at them but didn't comment. She said it was obvious he was "toxic" and from a "messed up" family, but his "bad boy" allure kept her hooked. She knew her time would be better directed towards her demanding job, and she was angry with herself about the amount of headspace men consumed. I wondered if the 'toxic' and 'messed up' labels actually belonged to her Family Soup.

She was smart and her career path looked rosy, yet she was filled with self-doubt professionally. In addition, her health was precarious and she often suffered chronic pain in her stomach. After several sessions and as she began to trust me and feel safe, she talked about the bullying that had happened at a previous workplace.

When someone is a victim of bullying at school or work, there has also often been bullying in the family. I asked her if the workplace bullying had a similar flavour to something she'd seen happen in her family and, if so, if it had been directed at her. At that moment, her solar plexus and stomach went into overdrive. Sunita was experiencing one of her excruciating but familiar stomach aches.

I invited her to relax as best she could, feel how the chair was supporting her and tune into her stomach, which seemed to be screaming to be heard. As she tuned in, I asked her to intentionally direct her breath into the pain. As she focused her breath, she was able to describe the colours, textures, feelings and sensations she was experiencing. Three distinct memories came rushing back to her. I was surprised there were three memories at once, but they were all linked. The very fact she was accessing three difficult memories showed me she was more than ready to acknowledge and work through the traumas held within the memories.

The first was a memory of her shock of being hit across the face by a male cousin who was 10 years older than her. She was 6 at the time and he was 16. The physical attack was followed by verbal abuse.

The second was a memory of another male cousin molesting her when she was around 10 years old. The third memory was when she was much older – 24. Her parents and older siblings wanted her to marry. They'd found her a "nice Indian boy" they thought would be a match for her. But Sunita wasn't ready to get married, nor was she remotely interested in the man that was being pushed at her.

She did her best to say no but was met with a barrage of outcries from her siblings. The same male cousins who had traumatised her as a child joined in the disapproval, threatening to sabotage her relationships at work if she didn't agree to marry. Her parents were also furious that she refused to acquiesce. In fact, everyone in the family was angry with Sunita when she stood her ground and said no to the match. She was threatened and manipulated by some family members and ignored by others, and her mother didn't speak to her for a year. Sunita described this time as "18 months of hell".

We worked through each trauma memory in separate sessions, focusing on supporting the adult she is now to speak up and protect her child within. It was difficult at first as she practised using simple but powerful words like 'stop', 'no', 'leave her alone', 'back off' and 'how dare you'. She practised speaking up to the perpetrators, owning her voice and declaring her right to her own choices. Realising she had a right to protect herself was a revelation since she had not been protected as a child. She thoroughly challenged her traits of powerlessness, passivity and the need for approval. These were Tricky Traits her mother had modelled when she'd done her best to remain married to Sunita's father.

Sunita quickly learnt to stand up for this vulnerable inner little girl and young woman. It became clear to her she was much more than a survivor: she was strong and capable and able to set clear boundaries with bullies and boyfriends. She saw the truth of her own immense power.

Sunita was also able to give her child within the safety and protection to allow this hurt child to express her sadness. She gave herself 15 minutes each day to either meditate or journal, to grieve all she'd had to deal with and to grieve the lack of compassion and safety she'd been shown in each of the three bullying experiences.

As she worked to empower herself and release the grief, Sunita found herself ending her relationship with her boyfriend. As she processed the layers of her trauma, she gradually recovered her self-worth and dignity. She concluded that she deserved consistency and respect from her boyfriends. This coincided with the offer of a promotion to associate director level and an offer to work at head office in a European capital city. She was thrilled and accepted the promotion and the transfer. She is currently dating a Spanish man and is discovering that both he and tapas are delicious.

Deep Dive
Nine Stages of Healing Trauma

The process of healing and integrating the emotional wounds that result from abuse and trauma can be challenging. It takes time and patience. However, it's an incredibly rewarding journey as you recover parts of yourself that may have been lost, including your inner Joy and expressive Juiciness.

Unexamined trauma takes up lots of space inside ourselves. To support your resilience, it is essential to fully own yourself and your reactions. Unless we process the trauma, we may continue to view life through a painful lens of trauma memories and limiting beliefs.

This Deep Dive is all about how to process a childhood trauma or recent trauma. It has been adapted from Dr Andrea Brandt's article '9 Steps to Healing Childhood Trauma as an Adult' in *Psychology Today* (see *Resources*). I have also recorded a meditation to take you through these healing stages, which you can access at andreaanstiss.com/juicylife. Before you use the trauma healing meditation, it's useful to read the stages to have a sense of the map of the territory we are exploring.

> Unexamined trauma takes up lots of space inside ourselves

Right now, the task is to become super curious about any trauma you may have experienced. Allow yourself to be comfortable. Have your pen and journal or writing device next to you. Remember to breathe deeply.

One: Grounding

For healing to work, we must be fully inhabiting our bodies and be in the present. I invite you to find a quiet space where you won't be disturbed. Close your eyes and take several deep breaths, bringing your awareness into your body. Feel your bottom on the chair or floor. Feel your back supported by the back of the seat. Feel the floor under your feet. Let yourself feel connected to the ground, the earth under you. Imagine a river of energy moving from your tailbone into the depths of the earth. This river of energy connects you with the solidity and safety of the earth.

Two: Recalling

Allow yourself to think of a situation that you have been disturbed about recently. A situation that triggered a mild to strong reaction. Or one that may have triggered a feeling of shock, numbness and disconnection. Recall what happened in as much detail as possible. Imagine, feel or sense yourself back in that time and space. Consider what you saw, heard, smelt, tasted and felt. Allow your emotions to begin to move in your body. Breathe deeply to support the flow of your emotions.

Three: Sensing

Continue your deeper breathing. Gently guide your awareness through your body. Be aware of your feet, your legs, your pelvis, your entire back including your spine, your belly, your diaphragm, your heart and lungs, your shoulders, arms, hands. Be aware of your neck and throat. Be aware of your head, face and scalp. Notice where your body is calling to you – perhaps there is an area of pain. Become aware of the sensations in your body. Noticing the sensations is a bit like exploring underneath the emotions to discover their physical roots. Notice sensations like tightness, pain, burning, gripping and tingling. Notice also an absence of sensations like emptiness, hollowness, numbness, or spacing out and disassociation. All of this is information that will help you process your experience. Take time to investigate and explore your physical sensations.

Four: Naming

Connect an emotion to each of the sensations you identify in your body. Perhaps the gripping in your chest can be named fear? Is the sensation of blocking at your throat terror? Maybe the heat in your knees is anger? Is the heaviness in your chest sadness? Take your time to name these emotions and notice the subtle but vital differences between them. For example, vindictiveness feels like anger that has become frozen. Resentment feels like constantly recycled anger. Rage feels like anger that is hot, explosive and ready to move. Refer to the Feelings List on my website (andreaanstiss.com/juicylife) to help you expand your emotional vocabulary. This work will support you in knowing more about your rich and complex self.

Five: Accepting

It's important to accept what we feel. If we don't accept our feelings we create fractures in our mind-body connection. We might ignore our feelings or criticise them the way we were ignored or dismissed as children. Whether it feels true or not to your conscious mind, practise saying out loud, "I accept myself for feeling hurt [or angry, anxious, sad…]." Repeat this affirmation of acceptance for all of your emotions. It is particularly important for the emotions that are judged as more shadowy or shameful such as rage, vindictiveness or humiliation. This stage opens the doorway to accepting all aspects of your humanness and loving yourself even for your challenging parts.

Six: Experiencing Fully

Stay with your feelings and sensations (we have already discussed the invitation to sit with feelings at the end of *Step 3* – here is this invitation again). Don't try to change them, minimise them or run from them. Notice and welcome any discomfort, pain or shame you feel. Allow your feelings to move and flow. Let your body respond spontaneously to the flow of feelings. Maybe you need to punch a pillow or cry on the floor, or scream. Follow the impulses of your wise body. Expressing emotions is essential in processing your feelings and the trauma.

Seven: Opening To The Wisdom

Do the feelings and sensations you are having right now remind you of one or more of your experiences or feelings from the past? Do they feel familiar? Do you sense a connection to an earlier trauma or a limiting belief about yourself? Ask a younger part of you to come forward from your imagination. This younger part, which we have already referred to as the inner child, may have something to share about this experience or another experience that occurred that was too overwhelming at the time to acknowledge or speak about. Listen to the messages.

Eight: Sharing

Use your journal to reflect on any insights or new perspectives you may have gained after doing these exercises.

* Describe what happened when the wounding experience first happened and how you dealt with it at the time.
* Write what you have now come to see about this experience. How has your relationship to the trauma event shifted?
* How has your relationship to yourself changed?

- Perhaps you can identify a limiting belief you have been viewing life through? Perhaps you feel more space? Or a little softer around your heart?
- Once you have reflected, I invite you to share your experience with a safe friend. This is a friend who will not shame you or question the validity of your experience. They will listen and simply be a kind witness.
- Use the raw feelings letter writing process we explored in *Step 2* and *Step 3*. This is a useful resource to further move emotions out of your system.

Nine: Letting Go

As a final stage, you may want to perform a ritual of letting go.

- Burn the letter you wrote to the person who hurt you.
- Take a journey to the ocean or a lake and immerse yourself in the water with the intention of releasing any remaining trauma into the water. Your bathtub filled with Epsom salts and essential oils is also useful for releasing using the elements of salt, water and plants.
- You can also simply sit and visualise or sense the energy the trauma took up inside you leaving your body. The earth is happy to receive and transmute this energy.
- The animal fable described in the pages below is another powerful letting go writing process.

> "Earth beneath me. Sky above me. Water within me. Air around me. I am okay."
>
> JENNIFER WILLIAMSON

WRITE YOUR LIFE

Writing is a powerful way to help you heal from traumatic experiences. It's helpful to write down what happened to you over your life or perhaps to just focus on one disturbing memory. Find a quiet space where you won't be interrupted. Get it all out on paper or on your laptop. You can decide whether to write it as bullet points or as a story. As you write, you may be better able to put the pieces together. Often our memories of frightening events become fragmented in our system. They become spread out and fractured, negatively colouring how we view our lives. Writing and speaking about our trauma helps us to give it a location so it doesn't poison all of our being. Writing can help us break our own silence, denial or minimising. When speaking the unspeakable feels too much of a stretch, writing the unspeakable is a great start. As you write, give yourself full permission to breathe and to grieve. Writing helps us to see the events from a different perspective and also gives the memory its proper place. We can recognise and accept it as a story and a memory, something that happened in the past and that belongs in the past.

THE ANIMAL FABLE

Writing your traumatic memory story and replacing people with animals is a technique that can help you feel more kindness towards the part of you that survived. The power differential between the perpetrator and the survivor is often made very clear with animal analogies. This opens the path for even more compassion for your inner child.

The characters in your story are represented by animals. Choose an animal that best matches how you experienced the people in your traumatic memory. For example, if you had a cruel schoolteacher, in your story she might become a grizzly bear with enormous claws. You might become the frightened rabbit who felt frozen as if caught in headlights every time the teacher attacked another child and you feared you might be next. Your friend, who was often bullied by the teacher and who became more timid each day, might become a baby koala bear – cute, but not really present. Once you have written your story and exchanged the main players for animals, read it aloud. You can light a candle to bring in a sense of the sacred and direct your voice to the candlelight (fire is a wonderful element of transmutation). You can read it to your safe friend or support circle. Reading your story aloud helps your pain be witnessed with kindness. You can allow this kindness to touch you as well as your inner child. This helps you to give the memory its rightful place, a memory that belongs in the past. Healing trauma creates more space for your Joy.

> "Your trauma is not your fault,
> but healing is your responsibility."
>
> ANONYMOUS

TLDR too long didn't read

- (JL) Trauma and its symptoms are things many of us experience as part of our human journey.

- (JL) Trauma research abounds and we now have a better understanding of how trauma impacts our nervous systems – and a broader choice of trauma healing approaches.

- Ⓙ️Ⓛ️ We want to repair our trauma symptoms and take back our power; otherwise, we will tend to repeat traumatic experiences.

- Ⓙ️Ⓛ️ There are four main ways our body responds to traumatic events: freeze, fight, flight and fawn.

- Ⓙ️Ⓛ️ The three Bs are the basic keys for healing trauma: 'Believing' it happened, 'Breaking' the silence and 'Banishing' the blame.

- Ⓙ️Ⓛ️ Behind a lot of traumas are multifarious abuses that can be difficult to name. These abuses include but are not limited to physical, sexual, emotional and spiritual abuse and neglect.

- Ⓙ️Ⓛ️ Use the tools of meditation, emotional processing and writing to heal trauma.

- Ⓙ️Ⓛ️ Find a great trauma therapist or healer you connect with to regulate your nervous system and reconnect you to your body, your inner knowing and lovability. When you are ready, you may wish to join a healing group. There are healing groups and circles where leaders and participants provide support for fellow trauma survivors.

STEP 6

CREATE YOUR BOUNDARIES

"Good fences make
good neighbours."

ROBERT FROST

Boundaries are lines or limits that you set for yourself that both define and protect you in body, mind and soul. If a person crosses one of these lines in your relationship with them, there are usually consequences in terms of intimacy or trust in the relationship. Boundaries allow for respect on both sides.

In the preceding Steps, you have worked hard to recover your True Self and, in turn, your Juiciness. Strong boundaries safeguard this hard work and further ensure that you have the space you need to express your True Self.

Boundaries are determined by two opposing forces: the need for *individuality* and the *desire to belong*. A boundary clarifies who I am (as an autonomous individual) and who *we* are (as a couple, family or team of colleagues, for example). In a healthy relationship, your individuality is not seen as a threat to the relationship.

For instance, if I want to spend time pursuing my own fitness goals or playing tennis or hanging out with my friends, my husband will be happy for me and I will not feel any guilt about the time away from the relationship. We will have negotiated our boundaries such that we both get the amount of time we need for ourselves as individuals as well as enough time together to meet our need to belong.

> In a healthy relationship, your individuality is not seen as a threat to the relationship

However, boundaries are not rigid and may ebb and flow depending on circumstances. Another example from my own life that demonstrates this fluidity is that as my husband has been dealing with illness,

I have chosen to spend less time pursuing my own travel adventures and more precious time with him.

As you will discover in this Step, our relationship to our own boundaries is inextricably linked with *co-dependency*. One of the key characteristics and challenges of co-dependency is people-pleasing. People-pleasing is undoubtedly a Tricky Trait that I encourage you to get radically honest about as we explore the topic of boundaries in the coming pages.

BOUNDARIES ARE YOUR BFFs (BEST FRIENDS FOREVER)

We need to learn how to 'do' boundaries because we are born into this world without any. Instead, we are born with powerful attachment needs that keep us close to our caregivers. This closeness is essential for our survival. However, as we grow, the need for the proximity of the warm bodies of our caregivers lessens and loosens. It's a steep path from utterly dependent newborn baby to independent adult! Issues arise when, as adults, we stay in that Trance of imagining we are still dependent infants. We may struggle to separate and develop our own individuality.

Why is this so important? Because to be successful in relationships we need a clear, differentiated 'me' and a separate 'you'. Not knowing where you end and the other begins stops a healthy coming together of people. Without boundaries we get swallowed up and lost in relationships.

What do boundaries look like?

Boundaries come in many forms. Here are some examples:

1. A mother who tries to force her small child to eat a specific amount of food is crossing the child's boundary. She can only be responsible for *what* the child eats, not *how much*. A mother who provides an array of healthy food and trusts that the child will eat what they need is allowing the process of separation to occur naturally by trusting the child's own innate wisdom and body intelligence (assuming, of course, that the child is not sick!).

2. Parents of a young adult child who loses their job may offer to support their adult child financially during the period of unemployment. If they decide to stop this support when the child finds a new job, they are creating a boundary. This boundary allows the adult child to become independent once again and also reminds them of their individual autonomy and ability to survive without the parents.

3. Your boss may ask you to take on some extra work although you are already being stretched to your limit. Saying no to the additional work because you know it would cause you too much stress or steal from your treasured family time is an example of setting a boundary. Looking after yourself in the face of a request from an authority figure is not something we are taught to do.

4. Your friend wants you to go to a dinner party but you aren't feeling well, so you let her know that you need to rest – you put your needs first despite knowing that you will disappoint her.

Because I'm a 'love bug', it always felt counterintuitive to me that I needed to learn boundaries. I was seduced, like many of us, by the idea that love is all you need. It wasn't just the Beatles who sold us this line. This false idea is fed by endless romantic myths: fairy tales, romcoms, pop songs, poems and marketing executives. Our boundary styles are learnt from how we saw our caregivers model boundaries and how they interacted with us. Boundary styles can also be influenced by a trauma that happened to us.

If your boundaries were ignored or invaded as a child, you will need to learn that you have a right to be safe. You have a right to dominion over your life.

Love, respect and clear communication require healthy, separate selves with clear boundaries. Healthy individuals are skilled at assertiveness, which is the truthful expression of their needs and wants.

BOUNDARY BOUNTY

Boundaries are an act of excellent self-care. We'll explore more about the benefits of boundaries later. If created and enforced well, boundaries will help to prevent you from:

* People-pleasing: feeling empty on the inside but acting pleasing on the outside
* Giving away your power
* Feeling impotent
* Feeling like a victim
* Falling into old behaviour
* Feeling intimidated
* Shutting down
* Going into shame
* Feeling violated, used and exhausted

> "'No' is a complete sentence."
> ANNE LAMOTT

PEOPLE-PLEASING PROBLEMS

People-pleasing is a giant Tricky Trait that undermines our value and steals our Joy. The 'disease to please' is also called co-dependency. It's an emotional, psychological and behavioural way of coping that we learnt as children. Co-dependency is rooted in the rigid rules of our family of origin, where emotions are seen as unacceptable. 'Don't feel, hide your feelings… you will be punished if you express feelings'. This underlying message is not just a way of being that appears in alcoholic or drug-addicted families, although this is where the term originates. The term 'co-dependent' was coined in the 1950s to acknowledge and support partners of alcoholics and chemical dependents who were enmeshed in the lives of those they cared for. Now we have a much broader definition where co-dependency has varying levels of severity.

Co-dependent relationships

Co-dependents often have poor self-concept and weak boundaries, including a difficulty having or expressing an opinion or saying no. The underlying Tricky Trait beliefs that co-dependents need to challenge are:

* My feelings are not okay.
* I am unlovable.
* I am alone.
* I don't matter.
* I am wrong.
* I must hide.

Here's an imaginary scenario illustrating how a person may develop the Tricky Trait of people-pleasing. A little girl, let's call her Houda, is told repeatedly by her mother:

"Shhh! Stop crying, Houda. You'll annoy Uncle Moneer."

Or,

"Houda, if you keep that noise up, I'll beat you up."

In this way, Houda learns that her feelings are not okay and that other people's feelings are more important than hers. Imagine how differently Houda would feel about herself if her mother had said this instead:

"Darling, I see you are sad. I'm here for you. Go ahead and cry. Get every single tear out. Here, have some tissues. Oh, and don't worry about Uncle Moneer, he's always a bit grumpy. Right now, fully expressing your tears is what I want to support you with, sweetheart."

Challenging the Tricky Trait of people-pleasing will help us create a strong sense of our unique selves, and this will allow us to engage in healthy and equal relationships. The 'disease to please' is rooted not only in our family conditioning but also brainwashed into us through the education we received in church, in our communities and at school.

As a little Brownie (part of the Girl Guide movement), I had to solemnly declare to Brown Owl, Tawny Owl and all the other Brownies that I would "do my best to do my duty to God, the Queen and the country". It felt like a huge responsibility and that I was way down the pecking order. This further invalidated the importance of my feelings and experience.

On the Hoffman Process, we often ask on the first day:

"Which of you had parents who told you or modelled for you: *Love yourself first, then look after others?*" Of course, no one raises their hand.

Putting others before ourselves, caring about the needs and feelings of others ahead of our own, is endemic in our society. No wonder so many of us need to actively learn how to have healthy boundaries and be told that it's okay to look after ourselves!

People-pleasing pointers

As a child, people-pleasing was how you secured love, attention and affection. It was a survival strategy. Becoming aware of this Tricky Trait and the havoc it now wreaks may inspire you to build strong, effective boundaries and enforce them. In defining your boundaries, based on your values and needs, you can connect with your own True Self and live a life full of Juiciness.

The people-pleasing pointers that follow were inspired by Anne Wilson Schaef, a co-dependence expert and bestselling author of *Co-Dependence Misunderstood-Mistreated*.

* Often a people-pleaser takes on the confusion, problems and emotions of others as their own. This is called the 'disease to please'. It's also referred to as the disease of co-dependence. It's called a disease because it profoundly impacts relationships. Since pleasers have few or no boundaries, they take on another's sadness, worry, joy or whatever people around them are feeling or thinking.
* People who have no boundaries tend to personalise whatever happens.

* People-pleasers tend to live from a place of 'What will people think?' Concern about how they are perceived by others controls much of their life. In order to feel safe and accepted, they spend a lot of time figuring out what others want and need, like and dislike.
* People-pleasers are often dependent on others for their right to exist, to take up space on the planet. They compulsively seek approval and validation from the outside. They have not yet learnt how to give that approval and care to themselves.
* People-pleasers also tend to dismiss their own perceptions of situations until they are validated by others. Even though they may be very intuitive, they may ignore their own knowing.
* People-pleasers are often caretakers. The 'taking' part of caretakers is important to acknowledge. People-pleasers often have little sense of their worth and may use caretaking as a way of feeling like they deserve to take up space.

> Often a people-pleaser takes on the confusion, problems and emotions of others as their own. This is called the 'disease to please'

Often they do for others what others can and need to do for themselves for their own growth. People-pleasers thus deprive others of their opportunities to learn and grow.

CoDA CURIOUS

Co-Dependents Anonymous (CoDA for short) is one of the 12-step programs available worldwide for people who want solid support to overcome their people-pleasing patterns. I encourage many of my clients to attend online or in-person groups. CoDA's program is a powerful way to transform the Sticky Tricky Traits of denial, low self-esteem, control and compliance that hold us back (see coda.org for details).

The Deep Dive questions below are inspired by 'The Recovery Patterns of Codependence', which is part of the free literature from the 12-step programme available via CoDA's website (see *Resources*). If you are suffering from this 'disease to please', you are likely to answer yes to many of these questions. I invite you to take the exploration further and reflect on the consequences of these patterns. CoDA's website is an excellent place to start.

Attempting to control, change or fix another person is a major hallmark of co-dependent behaviour. Another is betraying yourself and your needs in order to be 'chosen'. Co-dependent behaviours often result in you abandoning yourself as you fixate on another. Self-betrayal is the opposite of uncovering your Juiciness and revelling in your True Self.

Deep Dive
TRICKY TRAITS OF CO-DEPENDENCY

Gather your writing device or journal and respond to these questions on co-dependency. Remind yourself of the inner steps (*Awareness, Owning, Action*) before you journal. And remember to breathe!

Tricky Traits of denial
* Do you have trouble identifying what you are feeling?
* Do you minimise, alter or deny how you really feel?
* Do you cover up pain by using anger, humour or isolation?
* Do you recognise the unavailability of people to whom you are attracted?

Tricky Traits of low self-esteem
- Do you have trouble making decisions?
- Do you value others' approval of you over your own approval of yourself?
- Do you see yourself as a lovable and valuable person?
- Is it hard for you to admit mistakes?
- Do you have difficulty identifying and asking for what you need and want?

Tricky Traits of compliance
- Do you give up on your own values and compromise your integrity to avoid others' disapproval or rejection?
- Do you minimise your own interests to do what others want?
- Do you accept sexual attention when you really want love?
- Are you overly loyal, remaining in harmful situations for too long?

Tricky Traits of control
- Do you believe people are unable to take care of themselves?
- Do you use charm to convince others you are caring and compassionate?
- Do you use blaming and shaming to manipulate others?
- Do you pretend to agree with others to get what you want?
- Do you demand your needs are met by others?

Tricky Traits of avoidance
- Do you behave in ways that invite others to reject, shame or express anger towards you?
- Do you hide your feelings and needs to avoid being vulnerable?
- Do you imagine displays of emotion are a sign of weakness?
- Do you do the 'push-pull' (pull people towards you, but when they get close, push them away)?

As you learnt in the early Steps, you took on many of these people-pleasing Tricky Traits as a way to cope with your childhood. As an adult you now have the agency to make different choices.

Once you have identified your people-pleasing Tricky Traits, please return to the 'embodied letting go' suggestions in *Steps 2* and *3*. These will support you to take action to create some space between you and these traits.

> "Daring to set boundaries is about having the courage to love ourselves, even when we risk disappointing others."
>
> BRENÉ BROWN

THE NITTY-GRITTY OF BOUNDARIES

Now that we have explored what sorts of issues get in the way of you having – and then setting – clear boundaries, let's dive even deeper into the nature of boundaries. We'll look at the different types of boundaries and how they serve you. This is key, as good boundaries can absolutely transform your relationship with life and connect you to even more Joy.

Three types of boundaries

In this context, there are essentially three different types of boundaries: the boundary of *containment*, the boundary of *protection* and the boundary of *screening*.

Separating these can help us see more clearly which of them may benefit from either more enforcement or more flexibility. After I describe each boundary type, there are some reflection questions for you to journal about.

1. *Containment*

Boundaries help us to define or contain our sense of self. They help you know what is and is not you. Moment by moment, we have emotional, physical and mental experiences of ourselves. They are constantly changing. When we grow skilled at *containment*, we can deal with shifts in our inner world and take delight in who we are. We realise our inner world is always ebbing and flowing, and we allow this energy to move within. If you have a healthy sense of containment, then you will naturally also have respect for another's flow of feelings, opinions, thoughts and experiences. Similarly, if you have an unhealthy sense of containment, anything that does not conform to your emotions and perspective may register as a threat to your sense of self, or you may need to make the other person wrong in order to preserve your sanity.

Imagine you've been told your whole life that black clothing must be worn for funerals and that this is such a deep-seated belief in your culture that nobody ever questions it. Then you travel to a country where people wear white at funerals.

If you have a healthy sense of self, you might think, "Oh, how interesting! It turns out that black isn't always worn at funerals and that different cultures have different traditions. Travelling is expanding my perspective and helping me learn."

If you don't have a healthy sense of containment, it might shake you to your very core. "Are these people celebrating the fact that someone has died? If so, they must be extremely odd and possibly dangerous."

* Are you stuck in the 'same-same' routine?
* Do you keep people at a distance?
* Do you isolate?
* Do others experience you as rigid or abrasive?

3. *Screening (or filtering)*

While protection is about keeping us safe, *screening* is a boundary that allows nourishment in. When you have a balanced sense of screening, you'll be clear about what you need, and you'll have the ability to take it in and the self-awareness to know when you are satisfied.

For example, if you've had a chaotic day, being able to receive support is vital. That support may be a chat with your partner, a run on your own or with a friend, or a journaling session. Screening is not just about asking for and receiving the right kind of support, it's also an essential tool for knowing when you've had enough. Think of screening as discernment; it's the ability to know that you need something, the ability to identify what you need, and the ability to know when that need has been fulfilled. That 'enough-ness' extends to sex, food, affection, alcohol, friends, computer games, work, partying, shopping and exercise. *Screening* is the boundary that helps to regulate us and prevents us from over-doing and indulging in what may turn into addiction.

Reflect on these questions to explore your relationship with your screening boundary:

* Do you have difficulty regulating the amount of food, alcohol, drugs, screen time or sex you take in?
* Do you overextend yourself with exercise, social activities, relationships, spending money, work or volunteer work?

* Do you feel hopeless around setting limits for yourself?
* Do you often feel like you're bingeing on life but you're still not satisfied?

SIX POINTERS FOR HEALTHY BOUNDARIES

Before I outline specific steps and words to keep your boundaries strong, consider these six healthy boundary pointers:

1. *Clarity*

    Get clear on what you want and need in order to define your boundaries. You will need to listen carefully to your values and your commitment to self-respect and self-care. Clue: we often know exactly what our values are when our boundaries have been violated!

2. *Plan*

    Plan your boundaries in advance. When you know you are going into a potentially challenging situation, set your boundaries before you engage. For example, if you suspect that your boss is going to ask you to work late, decide in advance what you are willing to do and what you are not.

3. *Practise*

    Practise by writing out the words you will use, roleplaying and visualising your boundaries.

4. *Choose well*

    You always have a choice. Is it safe for you to be there?

5. *'No, thanks'*

    Practise saying no. It's possible to say no from the heart without aggression. If people ignore your no, follow the empowering steps below. Whenever we say yes when we mean no – and no when we really mean yes – we are abandoning and betraying ourselves. Recognise that self-betrayal is a replay of what happened when you were small. Don't do this to yourself.

6. *Time*

    Ask for time. We usually don't have to give answers immediately even if this is what the other says they need. Practise a stock response such as: "I need some time to think about this, I'll get back to you by [xyz date]." This buys you time to consider what action or response suits you best.

EMPOWERED ENGAGEMENT

By engaging differently you can stay empowered. When your boundaries feel threatened, try using an 'I' statement to say how you feel or experience the situation honestly. For instance, "I feel hurt and rejected when you shout at me," or "I experience you as not listening to what I am saying and that makes me feel like shutting down." Using 'I' statements means you are owning your experience, which is more truthful and powerful than blaming. Don't say, "You make me feel hurt and rejected."

Teach people exactly what you want by asking for it. Years ago, I attended a workshop called 'Money and You'. It was led by the now famous financial advice author Robert Kyosaki. My main takeaway from that workshop was: there is no harm in asking. Ask for what you want, always.

Here are some useful sentences:

* I want...
* I really appreciate it when you...
* Thank you for...
* I'm not prepared to...
* This works for me...
* This doesn't work for me...

Messy situations

My colleague and friend Lisa Laws, an addiction coach, outlines a three-step boundary approach when you are entering chaotic or toxic situations.

> Ask for what you want, always

Remember: you do not have to stay in toxic situations where you are being disrespected.

Three empowering steps

One: Ask for what you want
For example, "I don't want you to talk to me like that. When you say that, I feel..." If your request is ignored, move to step two.

Two: Set an ultimatum or give a warning
"I'm not prepared to listen to you speak to me like that. I'll leave if you won't calm down and continue to speak to me disrespectfully. I'm willing to speak to you if you are polite." If your warning is ignored, go to step three.

Three: Take time out
When all engagement tactics fail and your boundaries are disrespected, you may feel threatened or vulnerable, and then it would be smart to

withdraw. "I'm leaving now. I need to be alone right now. Let's talk about this again when we've both had a chance to calm down."

Kareem's story

Kareem grew up in a large and strongly religious family that valued community spirit, sharing resources and, above all, helpfulness. Kareem absorbed the traits of helpfulness and support of others but took it too far. His life was in emotional and financial disarray when we first spoke.

He had a history of saving people from financial disasters. He allowed a friend who was originally staying for a week to stay for a year in his apartment rent-free. He lent his car to another friend who failed to put water in it and seized the engine. The repairs cost Kareem enormously and also cost him the friendship. He lent money to friends and family members without any clear plan or contract about how they would repay him. Often they didn't bother to repay him, and Kareem felt awkward pursuing the money.

He was yet to uncover his Tricky Trait of boundary-less 'love buying' when he came to the rescue of his boss. His boss was in a dire financial situation, and Kareem had made some profitable investments on the surging crypto market. He decided he would cash in his crypto and lend his boss $2,000,000. His boss, gushingly appreciative, verbally assured Kareem the loan would be returned with excellent interest in less than six months. Kareem trusted his boss implicitly, even though he had only worked for him for a brief period.

His money was not returned after six months, although his boss promised it would be – soon. Three months later it was the same story: "soon". Meanwhile, most of Kareem's colleagues no longer had jobs in the company; the organisation Kareem was helping to prop up was collapsing around him.

Kareem's shocking disregard for his own financial future and his unquestioning trust in people who had yet to prove they were trustworthy were pointing to his non-existent boundaries and lack of self-care. Everyone else came first in Kareem's family: the religious leaders, the relatives, the friends, and the starving kids in the refugee camps.

As he unearthed his truth and his Tricky Traits, he became aware that his poor self-esteem led him to want to show his boss how smart and successful he obviously was. And of course, he could demonstrate this: he had the money available to lend. Although Kareem was smart, successful and conscientious, he was incapable of validating this for himself. Needing that approval from the outside cost him – literally.

It was then that Kareem took ownership of his Tricky Trait of 'love-buying' and came to understand why he'd wanted his boss's attention and approval. When Kareem was growing up, his father – busy working two jobs and attending to community responsibilities – had little time to give Kareem and his six siblings attention.

With Kareem facing the grim fact that he might never see his $2,000,000 again, we began some physical anger expression with a boxing bag. Kareem accessed his rage: it was well and truly alive under his Mr Helpful mask. In doing so, he used the energy this created to feel, define and strengthen his boundaries. He was an individual, not just a member of a tribe. He deserved to thrive and could also choose to be generous when appropriate without sabotaging his financial safety.

Getting in touch with anger and safely expressing it is essential for boundary setting. As we continued our sessions, Kareem could see how he'd allowed many people to take advantage of him and how co-dependence was in the fabric of his culture and his Family Soup.

Kareem started saying yes to himself and his own desires. He could see he was just as precious as the religious hierarchy, the relatives and the poor and needy. And just as he mattered, so did his money. He could respect money, nurture his investment talent and consider a future family with children who might benefit from and inherit his money. He could respect money, respect himself and still be generous.

To date, Kareem has recovered half of his money. More importantly, he has understood the value of his boundaries, his money and his own worth. He stringently and honestly evaluates his motivations when he feels compelled to lend money or give gifts.

TLDR TOO LONG DIDN'T READ

- ⓙ Boundaries are lines or limits that you set for yourself to define and protect you on multiple levels. Once understood and embraced, they will become your BFF.

- ⓙ Boundaries are created by two elements: our individuality and our desire to belong. We need to honour both.

- ⓙ Many of us are people-pleasers. It was how we secured love and attention as kids, but problems arise when we continue to do it as adults. Boundaries help us transform this 'disease to please' and take dominion of our own delight.

- ⓙ Co-Dependents Anonymous (CoDA) is a 12-step programme that helps people connect with their higher power and learn self-care and how to work effectively to transform seriously sticky Tricky Traits.

- ⓙ Three important boundaries are: the boundary of containment, the boundary of protection and the boundary of screening.

- ⓙ When asserting yourself – that is, expressing your wants and needs – take full ownership. Use 'I' statements rather than 'you' statements in order to avoid blame.

- ⓙ In potentially toxic situations, set and express your boundary clearly. If ignored, then give a warning or ultimatum. If you are disrespected again, you have the choice to ask for time and leave.

STEP 7

DITCH THE TOXIC SHAME

"Dance until you shatter yourself."

JALAL AL-DIN RUMI

You have worked carefully to identify and transform the Tricky Traits in relation to your childhood, your ancestors, your trauma and your boundaries. This is important and powerful work. Incredibly well done. You'll be glad to know we're almost there. But now we need to dive deeper into understanding the uncomfortable and unconscious dances we get caught up in with our fellow humans. By understanding the issues of both *shame* and *transference*, we can begin to rock 'n' roll with the world with more receptivity, rhythm and fun.

REACTIVITY OR RECEPTIVITY?

Any kind of relationship with a friend, colleague, lover or sibling can be confusing and button-pushing at times. Let's see what is really happening when we become hooked, triggered or we 'lose it'. We'll get to grips with our shame-based feelings and how they connect back to our trauma and exert a powerful block on our availability to dance with the world. We'll explore the fascinating movement of *projection* and *transference*. This occurs in a concealed way; as a result, we are often oblivious to our part in challenging relationships.

You will practise a process of 'growing yourself up' and identifying and meeting your own needs. As we evolve into open-hearted adults, we get to enjoy not just our own Juicy aliveness but everyone else's too. We become much less judgemental. As we transform our reactivity, we create the space for more Joy and delight.

OH SHAME!

Healing your *shame* is the single most powerful intention you can have to support yourself to live in your Juiciness and allow your True Self to touch the world. We all have shame, but mostly we don't want to recognise it, let alone work through it. It feels icky. Even hearing others share stories of their own shame can trigger our feelings of shame. Shame blocks our beautiful spiritual essence, our luminosity or our connection with our True Selves. Shame is the energy that triggers us to feel bad or toxic to the core, which is why we also call *it toxic shame*.

Shame triggers many uncomfortable feelings, feelings you may have already identified as Tricky Traits in the earlier Steps. Because of the darkness created by our shame, these feelings are worth repeating. They include:

* Self-hatred
* Disgust
* Unworthiness
* Disconnection
* Regret
* Self-consciousness

Shame gurus

Healing the shame that binds us, as pioneers John Bradshaw, Alice Miller and Brené Brown have highlighted, is a worthy practice in and of itself. Our shame beliefs create paralysing nervous system responses. Unhealed shame prevents us from being comfortable in our own skins. Shame causes our nervous system to freeze and shut down. It can also take us into fight or flight as a way to escape the intense feelings this powerful emotion generates. And often shame keeps us stuck in a Vicious Vortex of fight or flight, leading to freeze or fawn.

I invite you to embrace the fear of letting go of old perspectives, allowing *acceptance* to replace *shame* and *guilt*. This allows a space for wonder and magic to enter, a sense of innocence and playfulness. Transforming shame is about shifting the internalised shame that separates us from our own heart and the hearts of others; it restores our innate Joy and opens our connection with our True Selves.

> Unhealed shame prevents us from being comfortable in our own skins

Shame differs from guilt

It's easy to confuse shame and guilt, but they are not the same. Guilt is a sense that we have said or done something wrong or bad. It relates to our actions or behaviour. Shame is more hard-hitting. It is a wound at the level of our being. With shame, the feeling is I am wrong or bad. Shame causes us to doubt our basic goodness. Both guilt and shame deserve our utmost understanding and compassion to transform them.

An example of this might be forgetting your mother-in-law's birthday. If you feel guilty about it, you may feel some remorse or responsibility for the mistake. You can then apologise and perhaps buy her some flowers and put a birthday reminder in your calendar for next year. You can also be sure you're organised for Mother's Day and Christmas or Eid. And then you let it go. If you feel shame about this mistake then you may feel you are bad and worthy of contempt, and you may then expect to be berated by your in-law family and by your partner. Meanwhile, you are telling yourself what a hopeless daughter-in-law you are and feel as if you can never make this up to your mother-in-law. If others do berate you for your mistake, you may swallow whole their shaming messages, reinforcing your shame-based beliefs that you are disorganised, thoughtless and bad.

Toxic and healthy shame

Toxic shame differs from healthy shame. As Pia Mellody, an authority on co-dependency and love addiction, says in her podcast (see the link at andreaanstiss.com/juicylife), we need to know that our poop smells!

We need to know it's not okay to take off our clothes and run around naked at the mall, but it may be fine to do that in our bedroom. We learn these healthy shame boundaries when we are very young. If our parents or caregivers don't teach us about healthy shame, it's likely we'll experience toxic shaming consequences later.

If you, at the age of six, come home from a play-date with your friend's tennis racquet in your bag, it's important that your caregiver checks in about your newly acquired racquet. If it was given to you as a gift, that's fine, but if you took it because you wanted your own racquet, then your caregiver will teach you about boundaries and how we need to respect the difference between 'ours' and 'theirs'. You would be strongly encouraged to return the racquet and apologise for taking it. You may feel some *healthy shame* about your actions. This experience would teach you it's not okay to help yourself to your friend's tennis racquet, soccer ball or new shoes. You have learnt a valuable lesson about respect and boundaries. If your parents and teachers don't take the time to explain these social skills to you as you grow up, you may feel entitled to help yourself to more things that aren't yours. You may believe stealing is okay – because it wasn't challenged when you were small. And that may lead to close encounters with the people who enforce boundaries, such as hurt and disappointed friends, angry school principals or police, lawyers and criminal courts.

Toxic shame could occur if, on the other hand, you were beaten and yelled at for taking the racquet. If your caregivers shouted at you, "You are a devious and conniving thief," when really you just wanted to play tennis, you are likely to absorb those shaming messages and replay those messages to yourself.

Toxic shame is the shame that haunts us with a barrage of negative self-talk from the inner critic: "Who the hell do you think you are? You really are a defective, useless piece of shit. You are unlovable, inadequate, weak and unattractive." *Toxic shame* is the feeling that who we are is fundamentally no good and unlovable.

> **Toxic shame is the shame that haunts us with a barrage of negative self-talk from the inner critic: "Who the hell do you think you are?"**

Toxic shame makes us want to escape and hide, and addictive behaviours and substances become the means of escape. When we have a shame attack, we want the ground to swallow us up. Toxic shame makes us feel exposed, excruciatingly vulnerable and defective.

SHAME SOURCES

There are many reasons we may feel shame. As you read through the list below, check which ones resonate most with you. If you feel an emotional charge as you read, make a note of the shame source. We'll explore it further in the Deep Dive on befriending shame that follows.

Reasons we may feel shame

1. *Abuse and trauma*

   Abuse results in shame. People who abuse others act shamelessly, often dumping their own shame on others. Let's take a look at some examples of abuses that may have left a shame imprint on you:

   * EMOTIONAL ABUSE includes abandonment and neglect, teasing, name-calling and comparison. All other types of trauma, such as war, physical trauma, sexual abuse and spiritual abuse, contribute to emotional abuse and trauma.
   * PHYSICAL ABUSE includes beating, hitting, kicking, pinching and spitting.
   * SEXUAL ABUSE includes lewd comments, boundary invasions, inappropriate touching, underage or forced exposure to pornography, non-consensual sex and rape.
   * SPIRITUAL ABUSE includes being forced to follow a religion you don't choose or being judged for your religious or spiritual beliefs. It also includes being manipulated by a spiritual leader or hierarchy. All types of abuse and most unhealed trauma disconnect us from our spiritual cores. Look again at *Step 5: Identify and Embrace the Trauma*.

2. *Genetic and biological factors*

   We can feel shame about our body, our shape and our size. Eating disorders abound and impossible standards are created by diet culture marketers. We are shamed into shedding weight, exercising excessively and undertaking procedures like liposuction and gastric banding. We can feel shame about our skin colours, our ethnic origins or our countries of origin. We can feel shame about our gender and sexual preferences.

3. *Society's expectations and demands*
   We put expectations on ourselves to accomplish and achieve. This has its roots in the ideals and myths of our society and community. Those expectations also relate to gender, class and culture. If we fail to meet these standards, we may feel intense shame.

4. *Past or current relationships*
   Shaming relationships may have occurred as a child or teenager, or perhaps you are in one currently. Shame is generated in relationships by threats of abandonment or rejection. It is created by keeping secrets, perfectionism and over concern with public image. Disgusted looks, eye rolling, sighs or being ignored can create feelings of humiliation and shame.

DEEP DIVE
BEFRIENDING SHAME

Now take a deep breath. Shame is a challenging energy, and if the thought of all the things you feel ashamed about makes you want to run right now to your favourite addiction, I invite you to slow down and take another breath.

You can use this next Deep Dive to journal any toxic shame you may be carrying. Having digested the list of shame sources above, you may now be more aware of any shame you have experienced. Silence, secrecy and judgement are the three things shame needs to survive. Through writing we can break this silence and secrecy. Later you may choose to share this Deep Dive with a safe friend who will not judge or re-shame you. Know that we heal shame by sharing it with others who will not re-shame us. You will also want to grieve the losses that have resulted from the shame messages you uncover. And remember the three inner steps of *Awareness*, *Owning* and *Action* as you explore this Deep Dive into your shame messages.

Gather your pen and paper or note-taking device. Set aside some quiet time when you won't be interrupted. Have the tissues nearby. Let yourself break the silence, secrecy and judgement with yourself first.

Nine ways to shine a light on shame

Answer each of these questions in turn to learn more about how you might experience shame:

1. What comes between you and your complete love and acceptance of yourself?

2. What do you judge about yourself as shameful?

3. What do you judge about others as shameful? (This question helps you to see hidden judgements you also have against yourself. It helps you to see your projections.)

4. Who is shaming you now?

5. How were you shamed as a child?

6. Are you carrying shame from your parents or previous generations? See *Step 4, Recognise the Impact: Your Ancestors*.

7. How do you shame others?

8. What is the link between your shame now, the shaming you received as a child and the shame you put onto others and the world?

9. Find a safe and empathic friend or colleague to share your shame story with.

> "If we share our story with someone who responds with empathy and understanding, shame can't survive."
>
> BRENÉ BROWN

STOP THE SELF-SHAMING

I come from New Zealand, where 'tall poppies' – successful people who stand out from the norm – are strongly discouraged. Anyone who becomes a tall poppy is encouraged to be radically humble in order to compensate. I remember walking to a charming restaurant some years back to celebrate my dad's 90th birthday. I was flanked by two elderly relatives. One of them passed a compliment about my height. I was wearing heels and am relatively tall anyway. I laughed and explained how tall I was without the heels. The other relative, an uncle, suddenly berated me for delighting in this moment of celebrating nothing more than my height. I remember feeling rather shocked and shamed. It was like I was a five-year-old girl enjoying myself far too much. That incident highlighted the depth of the tall-poppy conditioning my uncle had (literally, in this case), which he was projecting onto me. Fortunately, that shame didn't stick to me; I was quick to identify the shame dynamic at play. I also like my height and love my heels! This kind of problem arises when we swallow whole any shame messaging directed at us – something we do as children because we are wired to believe that adults must be right.

TRANSFORMING SHAME MESSAGES – SIX QUESTIONS

Let's challenge some of the shame messages you may be using to keep yourself small and hidden. Once challenged, I encourage you to create a ritual to release these shame messages – so they no longer disconnect you from your innate worthiness and spiritual self.

1. What are the shaming messages I give myself?

2. What am I doing or feeling when I give myself this message?

3. Where or from whom did I get this message?

4. How old was I when I adopted this message?

5. What positive decision or statement do I need to make to change this message? Rewrite decisions you may have made like 'I am bad' or 'I am rotten to the core' to 'I am lovable, all parts of me are lovable' and 'I have a right to feel good about myself'.

6. Is there a ritual or action you would like to use to symbolise and deepen your sense of letting go of your shame? For example, you could write the old shame messages on paper and burn them. If you are able, please find a safe person to share your story with.

SLIPPERY SHAME

There are some controversial themes that recur as trouble spots of toxic shame. Let's call them the Big Four: Money, Sexuality, Love/

Attention and Addiction. Each of these Big Four is deserving of a Deep Dive. The reason I'm introducing these, while our eyes are wide open to shame spotting, is that these 'biggies' may well be contaminated by *shame residue*. These Big Four are organically connected to how we dance with the world. Consider how your shame beliefs have impacted your relationship to prosperity, sexuality, love and addictions.

Money

* What is your relationship to money?
* What shame-based feelings or beliefs do you have around your wealth or lack of it?
* How easy is it for you to give and receive money?
* Are there any shame-inducing events that occurred around money, wealth or ownership in your family's history? Examples are losing the family business because of bankruptcy, gambling or drinking away the family's savings, or gaining wealth through illegal trading.
* What shame residue have you been carrying around money?
* Who would you be and how would you act if you released shame around money and success?

Sexuality

* What is your relationship to sex?
* What shame-based feelings or beliefs do you have around your sexuality?
* How easy is it for you to give and receive sexual connection?
* Are there any shame-inducing events that occurred around sexuality in your family's history? Examples: your uncle having affairs with multiple women, your mother having a secret affair with her boss for a decade, or your mother being unable to forgive herself after having several terminations before you were born.
* What shame residue do you carry around sexuality?

* Who would you be and how would you feel if you released shame around your body and your sexual desires?

Love and attention

* What is your relationship to giving and receiving love and positive attention?
* What shame-based feelings or beliefs do you have around giving and receiving love and attention?
* How easy is it for you to give and receive attention?
* Are there any shame-inducing events that occurred around love and attention in your family of origin? Did you grow up where the 'tall poppy syndrome' demanded you keep small and hidden? Did your parents lose a parent at a young age and suffer from neglect? Was there any severe religious conditioning in your family, where the human need for love and attention was judged as 'spoiling'?
* What shame residue do you carry around your need to give and receive love and attention?
* Who would you be and how would you feel if you knew that everyone, including you, deserves love, attention and affection?

Addiction

* Addiction is the activity or substance we use to manage, escape from or numb our pain. Addictions are a symptom of our unhealed trauma and pain. We use addictions to avoid feeling our shame and pain but in doing so we create more shame feelings. Does this resonate with you?
* What are your addictions? Take some courage and time to name them.
* What is the pain or shame you may be attempting to avoid with your addictions?

* How may they contribute to your shame?
* What do you fear would happen if you gave up some of your addictions?
* Who would you be and how would you feel if you no longer acted helplessly and compulsively around your addictions?

> "Transference is multi-layered and complex and happens when the brain tries to understand a current experience by examining it through the past."
>
> MAKARI

PROJECTING LIGHT AND DARKNESS

Now you are aware of how shame impacts your sense of worthiness and belonging, let's look further at how projection and transference have a powerful but little-understood influence on our relationship with the world.

Projection is where we make up all kinds of beliefs and assumptions about others. In projecting, we look at the world through the distorting filters of our own suppressed or hidden energies. This is why we are doing so much work to root out our concealed beliefs, thoughts and feelings. When we project – which occurs without awareness – we assign responsibility for our feelings to other people or situations. We mistakenly imagine they are the cause of our (shitty or amazing) experience. In projection, the difficult feelings we have, often ones we least want to admit to, may be attributed to others.

For instance, if you've pushed your anger down, you may have a sense that the world 'out there' is the cause of your anger. Here's an example of one of my own Sticky Tricky Traits around projecting my disowned anger (you may relate!):

"That ignorant freak of a driver – who the hell does he think he is in his 'big W' Porsche?" I rant to myself, grinding my teeth, desperate to raise two fingers while leaning on the horn. The driver I'm cursing has failed to indicate and veered into my lane, narrowly missing the right side of my car. It's a very common occurrence in any hectic city, and I have plenty of opportunities to project my feelings at the 'freaks' who in the rush hour become the misplaced cause of and object of my rage. That driver becomes the symbol of any person in my history who's knowingly or unknowingly cut me off, cut in front of me or ignored me.

Road rage is just one of our socially acceptable ways of 'doing' anger. Shouting at the shop assistant because he doesn't have the brand of cigarettes or crisps you want is another. Cursing the security guard because he made you wait your turn. Belittling your partner because she misheard you... the list goes on. As we look further, we may discover we have a ton of accumulated anger sitting in our throat, jaw and lower back that's desperately seeking release. That anger has been gathering for a lifetime, but because we have been told to be a 'nice' girl/boy, we have never found an effective way to deal with it. Shouting obscenities in the car surrounded by tons of metal and raising the finger at drivers we hopefully won't see again becomes the habitual but uncool and disrespectful way to express that anger.

If we do the maths, we could attribute 20% of our reaction to the current situation and 80% to our history, where we learnt early on that the honest expression of anger was totally unacceptable in the family.

20% 80% check

When we are in reaction, the '20% 80% check' is an excellent reminder that the heightened emotions and the accompanying drama are not just about this upsetting moment. The upset has triggered a disproportionate response where the memories and unprocessed emotions of a similar flavour are rattled.

It's useful to ask how much of your reaction is about this moment and how much is about unfinished experiences in your history you perceive to be similar. The 'Growing yourself back up' Deep Dive later in this chapter will help you work through your reactions.

Befriending our shadow traits

Reactivity to the mother-in-law is another classic example. Complaints and jokes about the in-laws abound. You may experience your parent-in-law as highly judgemental and particularly critical of you. But as you pay attention more closely, you notice that, actually, *you* are very harsh on yourself, despite the fact you're aspiring to be compassionate to all beings. You are *projecting* your critical part onto your parent-in-law. The shocking fact is we often judge others for the very qualities we have disowned or disavowed in ourselves.

The only way to resolve any *projections* we are making is by taking ownership of our feelings, feelings that we may be acutely uncomfortable with. Some of those feelings could be well hidden, in what we call the 'shadow aspect' in therapist-speak. These are the parts of ourselves we would not want others to see or know about us. Often we see our shadow in other people but are blind to the same shadow living in ourselves. One example is control or manipulation. We are often aware of feeling controlled and manipulated by spouses, bosses, politicians or the tax department. It's more difficult to see how we can be controlling and manipulative to ourselves and others. Once we have identified these difficult feelings, we can find healthy and effective ways to befriend them – and then move the powerful charge of those feelings out of our bodies using the 'embodied letting go' suggestions in *Step 2* and *Step 3*.

Shadow traits

Here are some examples of shadow traits that we may notice in others but often struggle to own in ourselves. These darker or 'icky' Tricky Traits may be uncomfortable to admit to. Check if any of these shadow traits ring true for you. As you identify a trait, ask yourself the four questions:

1. How did I learn this Tricky Trait as a child?

2. How do I act this trait out in my life now?

3. What are the costs and consequences of this shadow trait in my life?

4. Do I want to continue with this Tricky Trait in my life or do I want to let it go?

Typical shadow traits are:

Arrogance
Bitterness
Clinging
Control

Entitlement
Fear of abandonment in relationships
Fear of suffocation in relationships
Greed
Hate
Hypocrisy
Lying
Miserliness
Perfectionism
Pretension
Promiscuity
Sarcasm
Slyness
Vengefulness

TRICKY TRANSFERENCE

Transference is where feelings about a person, usually the mum or dad of our childhood, are redirected to an entirely different person. This is a phenomenon experienced in our daily life of interactions and relationships. Transference shows up most in our close relationships and is created from a mix of memories, emotions and unconscious energies that are hidden from our everyday awareness. Transference was once considered part of therapy language, where we are transferring early relationships onto a therapist. But in truth, we can have transference with anyone and at any time.

A classic example of transference is how we react to people we perceive to have more authority or power than we do. With people in authority, we transfer an image of Mother or Father onto them, and we become smaller and with less power, while we imagine them to be bigger and with greater power. We are seeing this person through the distorted lens of our childhood experience with our caretakers.

Our transference is rooted in our earliest pre-verbal emotional development. We often – automatically and compulsively – react to others the way we learnt to react to our mother, father or caregivers as little ones. And those reactions can get us into all sorts of trouble! This is where we see adults throw tantrums and/or punches, swear, act out with alcohol, drugs or promiscuity or buy expensive cars or bags they can't afford. In transference, we may also react with helplessness, collapse and giving our power away.

A coaching or therapeutic relationship is a safe space to shine the light of awareness onto how you 'do' transference in your relationships. A mutually caring relationship with a friend or partner is also a great way to explore this if you both have the same intention about awakening to your habitual transference. By simply naming some of the ways we do transference, we can wake up to how we create our own experiences of reality. In awakening to and understanding the roots of our transference, we can access more of the clarity and integrity of our True Selves. When we release our distortions and judgements about others, we experience greater *spaciousness*. Spaciousness is where we are not identified with our Tricky Traits alone. It's where we are able to remain calm as that driver 'who must be in an awful hurry' cuts us off, rather than reacting with clenched fists and swear words.

There is greater space between us and our reactions or coping mechanisms. It's possible to step back and not take everything personally when we are aware that transference is often at play. In creating more spaciousness, our True Selves are effortlessly present. We can clearly see ourselves and celebrate others without the blind spots our transference creates.

Four types of transference

Being aware of your transference and resolving it majorly transforms how you experience yourself. There is immense freedom in seeing what's really going on in our relationships and how we may be 'setting it up' with our unconscious transference. Various kinds of transference are likely to be playing out in our lives. Below, I have outlined some of the usual types of transference. Read through these examples, holding in mind a challenging relationship, and notice which ones resonate:

1. *Father transference*
   We connect the characteristics of the father of our childhood with someone else, perhaps an authority figure such as a boss, teacher or therapist. This can show up as admiration, loyalty or imagining the person is wise and all-knowing. Or conversely, we may experience fear or anxiety depending on how our relationship was with our dad.

2. *Mother transference*
   This is similar to father transference but the person at the root of the transference is your mother or early female caregiver. This transference could arise with a friend, a colleague or someone who is in a position of authority. Mother transference can generate feelings of trust and nurturance. Or if your relationship with your mother was challenging, you may have feelings of frustration, hurt, or I-need-more-attention/time from the person you are transferring Mum onto.

3. *Sibling transference*
   This kind of transference may show up especially with our peers or colleagues when we are working or playing in team situations.

This reflects the relationships we had with our brothers and sisters. I am the only girl in my family and have four fun-loving, caring brothers. As a result, I mostly have a positive brother transference. In work and team situations, I often feel quite comfortable socialising and working with the men because my experience as a child with my brothers was good. If you have grown up with siblings who bullied you and you have yet to heal that experience, you may have a more guarded transference onto your team or colleagues.

4. *Guru/God transference*

    This kind of transference happens with students, disciples, followers and groups. Here, the leader or teacher, often a charismatic figure, is invested with all kinds of powers by the followers. Students project their individual power and light onto the leader and often set themselves up for manipulation or abuse. One recent example is Bikram Choudhury, the yoga teacher who was once at the top of a huge yoga empire. He is now on the run from students who have been suing him for sexual assault and harassment. He is said to be hiding out in Mexico, where his passport has been seized. His fleet of 22 luxury cars is now being sold off and will cover only a fraction of his debts.

Positive transference

As you can see from above, not all transference is where so-called negative aspects of ourselves are attributed to others. If, growing up, you didn't have permission to celebrate the beautiful, artistic, intellectual or powerful aspects of yourself, you will likely project those qualities onto others.

"Oh, that teacher is an absolute genius," says my friend Soraya, who has a PhD and two Master's degrees. She herself is a genius but can only see genius 'out there' in the other professors. She doesn't allow herself to recognise her own brilliant intellect because her parents encouraged her to keep really quiet about her 'smarts'. She was raised in a traditional environment where women were supposed to be subservient to men in every way.

DEEP DIVE
GROWING YOURSELF BACK UP

This is a Deep Dive you can use over and over to explore and process the triggers and transference that are underneath a painful situation in your life. It may be a current situation, a recurring situation or a past experience.

Start with a recent experience, something that has an emotional charge for you. The intention of this Deep Dive is to grow yourself back up into an adult rather than remain in the emotional reactivity that has its roots in the difficult experiences of your childhood or teen years.

Remember the three inner steps of *Awareness*, *Owning* and *Action*. Remember also to breathe deeply.

Bring to mind a recent or 'in the moment' upsetting incident involving another. It may be a work colleague, a friend or your partner. As you respond to the questions, write quickly, without editing what you are feeling and thinking.

Five questions to grow yourself back up

1. Does this difficult experience remind you of anything or anyone from the past or any events that happened to you?

2. What would you have liked to have said or done in this situation that you were not able to express?

3. What would you have liked them to have said or done, ideally, in response to what you expressed?

4. How are you feeling right now?

5. Reflecting on question 3, how can you give to yourself – in a caring way – what you wanted the other person/s to say or do?

Now pause to check if you feel complete with the process. If you'd like to explore further, proceed to the next round:

1. Go further back in time: memories or more details may have emerged from question 1 above. Does this difficult experience remind you of anything or anyone or of events that happened earlier in the past? Perhaps an experience with Mum, Dad, some of your siblings or early caretakers?

2. What was the incident or experience? What would you have liked to have said or done in this situation that you were not able to express?

3. What would you have liked for him or her to say or do, ideally, in response to what you expressed?

4. How are you feeling right now?

5. Reflecting on question 3, how can you give to yourself, in a caring way, what you wanted the other person to say or do? What was the nurturing self-care or re-parenting that you needed? What wise words?

> "Since the beginning of time, people have been trying to change the world so they can be happy. This hasn't ever worked, because it approaches the problem backward. What The Work gives us is a way to change the projector – mind – rather than the projected."
>
> BYRON KATIE

Sina's story

Sina felt defective and worthless as a human being and a woman. She attributed her intense feelings of shame to her truth that she was gay. She was raised in a culture where codes of sexual expression are strictly prescribed by law and religion. Growing up, Sina preferred girls to boys, which made her feel awkward and like an outsider. She had zero interest in talking to guys on the phone or sneaky meetings at the mall, which were the usual topic of giggles and bonding among her schoolmates. Her sexual preference had never changed, even though she'd prayed it might as it would make living in her society much easier. And now she had fallen in love with a woman she'd met online and who was from a radically different culture.

Alcohol became Sina's way of taking the edge off her feelings of shame and loneliness. Prescription painkillers also became a habit when she discovered they numbed emotional pain along with physical pain. Using alcohol contributed further to her shameful feelings: it was another rebellion against her culture's code of conduct.

Sina's love affair had to be hidden from her family. Her cousin had been sent away to a 'conversion' camp – his family had paid for 'therapy' to have him change his mind about his homosexuality. Based on the humiliation and trauma she understood her cousin had experienced, Sina knew she would need to keep her sexual preferences and her feelings for her beloved silent.

In our sessions, Sina put many thoughts and feelings on the table for exploration, including the impossibility of telling her mother this giant secret and the terror and foolhardiness of 'coming out' publicly in a climate that had little tolerance for sexual diversity. We also spoke about her enormous love for her family and the sacrifices her parents had made to provide her with a high standard of education. Sina was also aware that being open about her sexuality could influence how far she would be promoted in her job. The bottom line was that she felt totally rejected and shamed by her culture because of her sexuality. She recognised how a part of her was colluding with the rejection of her truth by abusing painkillers and alcohol, which only added to the sense of rejection.

I invited Sina to attend a small group I was facilitating called 'Rebonding of the Body'. This programme is a well-researched and effective healing process for individuals who have experienced a wide range of traumatic experiences, including survivors of abuse, cancer surgery and traffic accidents. It's been found to be especially useful for people with body image issues, depression, low self-esteem and toxic shame. The programme was created by my mentor, Dr Deanna Mulvihill, a pioneer in the field of trauma transformation.

We used a variety of healing modalities over the six sessions, including creative expression, storytelling, movement meditations and mindfulness. However, I imagined it would be the group connection that would serve Sina the most. Breaking the silence to people who won't re-shame us is potent medicine. In this confidential and supportive space, I wanted to help Sina become comfortable in her own beautiful skin with her own sacred choices.

Sina was indeed able to receive the unconditional listening and support the other participants offered her, and the Rebonding of the Body group remained in touch after we finished the programme. Sina's new healing network led her to discovering an underground gay community that overlapped into an artsy and spiritual healing group. These new friends gave her the love and acceptance she yearned for and permission to delight in her own choices. In this space, Sina was able to feel her own goodness, beauty and essential 'okay-ness'. There was plenty of support in this rich community to explore her own authentic spiritual connection.

Three years after we first met, Sina told me she'd made the decision to move to her partner's country – so she could complete her Master's degree and also so they could be free to explore their relationship in an open environment. She was heartbroken to leave her family but knew she had to follow her own unique path.

TLDR TOO LONG DIDN'T READ

- ⒿⓁ Shame-based beliefs/feelings and our unconscious ways of projecting and transferring our unexamined history onto others will interrupt our connections with the world.

- ⒿⓁ Toxic shame is a difficult energy. We avoid examining it because when we get close to it, we'd rather not! We use a number of strategies to avoid feeling our shame, including our addictions.

- ⒿⓁ Shame is projected onto us by people who behaved thoughtlessly or shamelessly. The roots of our shame come from abuse, trauma, family rules, ancestral wrongdoings and current shaming relationships.

- ⒿⓁ Shame has an unspeakability to it. We heal it by owning it, naming it and sharing it with people who will receive our story with empathy and understanding.

- ⒿⓁ We continue the cycle of shame by shaming ourselves, primarily through the voice of the inner critic and by projecting the shame onto our relationships with others. Sex and intimacy, money and success, love and attention and our addictions are particularly vulnerable to our shame-based beliefs.

- (JL) The mechanisms of projection and transference have a massive impact on how we see and relate to the world.

- (JL) A strong reaction to something is a clue that we are usually doing projection and transference. The 80/20 rule reminds us that 20% of our reaction is based on the present moment, and the majority of our overreaction is related to unprocessed emotions from the past.

- (JL) Projection is an assumption or belief that others have similar thoughts and experiences as you.

- (JL) Transference is the process by which needs and emotions originally associated with our early caregivers are unconsciously shifted to another person.

- (JL) It's important to grow yourself into an adult by examining how you can easily regress into that unseen lost child in the midst of your own transference and also when others transfer onto you.

- (JL) There are two key questions to ask your inner child. What does this little one need that they didn't receive? How can you give that to them in a caring way?

STEP 8

EMBRACE THE JUICY LIFE

"Yesterday I was clever, so I wanted to
change the world. Today I am wise,
so I am changing myself."

JALAL AL-DIN RUMI

Congratulations! What a trip. You've been on a journey through the rocky terrain of the conditioning into which you were born. You've identified and worked with your Tricky Traits to remove their charge and to make some empowered choices. You've acknowledged the play of your ancestral lineage and the burdens you may have carried for them. By your very awareness, you have lightened that load. You've explored your trauma and your nervous system responses. You are awakening to the reality that it is *you* who is holding on, and it is now safe to let go. If you need professional support around transforming your trauma, I wholeheartedly encourage you to set that up – please refer to the *Resources* section at the end of this book, where I have listed some trauma-informed therapists.

You have understood that boundaries are practical and necessary for protecting your integrity and space. You've dived courageously into shame. And you've wrestled with the power of projection and transference. As a result, your lens on yourself and how you view the world is wider. And you may also be feeling a little empty! There may be a question lurking in the back of your awareness: "Who am I now?"

Now, as we contemplate the *Who am I now?* question, we'll look first at the positive inheritances you received from your family, community and culture. Among the difficulties are the gems you received from your parents, the people who gave you life. Beyond the wounds of your childhood, there is a magical part of you we call the *wonder child*. We will look more closely at this later. Connecting with your wonder child opens you to innocence, fun and freedom. There is also this physical body, so often taken for granted, this feat of miraculous

> Connecting with your wonder child opens you to innocence, fun and freedom

engineering, this mammalian physicality that makes your being here possible and deserves your love and appreciation. Also in this Step, we will explore responsibility and accountability. And finally, we will contemplate how – via your unity with all of life – your True Self, with its Juicy radiance, nourishes the world.

YOUR UNREPEATABLE LOVELINESS

You are trekking this psycho-spiritual landscape to remember how ass-kickingly amazing you are. To remember the Joy that is an organic expression of your True Self. When I work with clients and we connect with their wounded inner children, I teach them how to speak lovingly to these lost little ones. I teach them how to be kind and caring in their language with themselves. We open our hearts to this little girl or boy and all they have so resourcefully survived. I remind them of their preciousness, their intrinsic value and their inner and outer beauty. I remind them they are worthy of love, appreciation and attention. I am reminding you too now! You *are* the beloved you have spent your life searching for. You are a unique beloved because there never was, nor will there ever be, another exactly like you. You are a delight in your own singular category.

Here are some statements to remind your neural pathways of some important truths. You may want to look at yourself in the mirror in the morning after you brush your teeth and speak these sentences aloud. You can also record on your phone the statements that most resonate with you and play them just as you wake up, as well as before you sleep. These are the two times of day when you are most open to receiving and assimilating fresh ideas. You could even chant these statements as prayers or sing them on your way to work in the morning.

Fresh statements to deepen your connection to your True Self

* I am a delight.
* I permit myself to fully embrace my True Self.
* I permit myself to fully express my Juiciness.
* I grant myself Joy, over and over.
* I lovingly parent myself.
* I am lovable.
* I grant myself abundance, over and over.
* I bask in my own splendour.
* I hold a special place in my heart for myself.
* Creativity is my birthright. I claim my power to choose.
* I respect myself and I deserve respect.
* I love asserting myself.
* I celebrate my beauty.
* I honour my body's needs for movement and stillness.
* I am blessed in many ways.
* I am a blessing.
* I am magnificent.
* I see the world with eyes of compassion.
* I easily say, "No, this doesn't work for me".
* Boundaries are my spirit animal!
* I let go of what's not working.
* It is safe to grieve.
* I am powerful and wise.
* I am proud of myself for surviving.
* I endured and now I enjoy.
* I am open to pleasure in all forms.
* Wealth, prosperity and abundance flow through me.

- I am good.
- I release guilt.
- I release old stories and identities.
- I have the discipline to set myself free.

Questions to deepen your connection to your inner child

- How are you, little one?
- What do you need (to feel happy, healthy and whole)?
- How are you feeling *really*?
- What are you tolerating that is no longer okay?

Maybe some of these sentences or questions resonate with you. Or perhaps you need to create some of your own affirmations. Go ahead! Ideally, healing affirmations need to be in the present tense. They can be in the 'I' or 'you' form, or in the first person using your own name as a salutation. For example: "Andrea, I'm so proud of you for saying no and taking some time to do what you really wanted to do."

> Healing sentences or affirmations seem like basic tools, but they help us recalibrate how we speak to ourselves

Healing sentences or affirmations seem like basic tools, but they help us recalibrate how we speak to ourselves. They are a powerful way to befriend and re-parent ourselves.

Deep Dive
RECEIVING GRACE FROM MUM AND DAD

In *Steps 2* and *3* you explored the Tricky Traits that challenge you in fully connecting to expressing your True Self. You have taken time to acknowledge and release the resentment, sadness and anger you may have felt towards your parents or caregivers.

Now we want to turn the tables and view our mother and father with appreciation and gratitude for the life they gave us. Now it's time to bring balance to this exploration by contemplating the beauty and grace you received directly from them.

As you explore this Deep Dive into appreciating Mum and Dad, remember the three inner steps: *Awareness, Owning, Action.*

Appreciating Mum and Dad

Spend some time sitting quietly, reflecting on how your parents or caregivers tried to be good parents or carers. What were their positive intentions? How did they positively contribute to your life and your Joy? Reflect on these themes in your journal if they are true for you.

* How did your parents create celebration or special times in your life – such as family birthdays, graduations, Ramadan or Christmas?
* How were you supported with schoolwork and study?
* How were your interests and hobbies encouraged?
* How were you cared for when you were sick?
* How did they make efforts to feed, clothe and shelter you?

* How were you encouraged to be physically active and/or honour your body?
* How did your parents support the expression of your creativity or uniqueness?
* Were there holidays, road trips or adventures you went on with your family?
* What skill sets were encouraged by your parents, such as visiting the library, learning a different language or being smart with money?
* How did your parents offer you emotional or financial support?

For example, as I reflect on these themes, I can identify many brilliant and beautiful inheritances from my parents. Both my parents were sporty. They encouraged me to join in ten-mile runs. My dad arranged long hikes where we trekked the forests and beaches of New Zealand with our extended family. Both my parents played tennis, and my mother encouraged my interest in tennis, which continues to bring me enormous Joy, incredible friendships and sore knees! My mum also took me to yoga when I was a teenager, and this spurred my lifelong interest in yoga, meditation, breathwork and India. My father loved reading about different cultures, and although he didn't have the opportunity to travel as much as me, he had a genuine interest in my travels and expatriate life.

Both of my parents had active social lives with their friends and stayed on good terms with the extended family. They both volunteered their time and expertise for causes they believed in and encouraged me to do the same.

For these phenomenal gifts, I am truly grateful. This is just a handful; there are many.

DEEP DIVE
RECEIVING GRACE FROM YOUR CULTURE

Via your parents, you were born into a community and a culture. Your culture also includes your early religious or spiritual influences.

Spend time contemplating the positive inheritances of your early community and culture. Write those appreciations in your journal or note-taking device.

Appreciating your community and culture

- Were there any spiritual or religious organisations where you grew up that supported you in a positive way?
- If you grew up somewhere where household help was usual, were there any nannies, maids, tutors or drivers who contributed to your life in a positive way?
- Were there any adult neighbours, teachers or leaders in your community who 'got' you? These are people who saw you, listened to you and mirrored you in a healthy way.
- Were there places in your community where you could enjoy nature – trees, parks, places to run or to ride your bike, places to swim? Were there times you felt awed by nature as a child?
- Was there anything particularly significant about the values of the community you grew up in? How do those values continue to support you?
- What are the gifts of your ethnicity or your indigeneity? If you moved countries, what are the gifts of your adopted country?

WONDER CHILD

Your wonder child is the part of you that is revealed after you have done the hard work of reclaiming your lost or wounded inner child. The term was coined by John Bradshaw, author of the phenomenal book *Homecoming*. John Bradshaw was hugely influential in bringing inner child healing to popular audiences in the 80s and 90s. He views our wonder child as the part of us that is "naturally religious" as this aspect of us knows without doubt that they are connected to something greater. This part of us is spontaneous, playful, lives in the here and now and is happy to experiment. Our wonder child connects us to our creative power. What creative urges live within you that are seeking expression?

Take some time to journal the following: *If I was to allow my creativity out, I might...* Let yourself write freely and include ideas that might seem impossible!

Examples of *wonder child* inspired creative impulses

* Sell everything, move to Peru to explore shamanic practices.
* Go hot air ballooning next Sunday morning.
* Make a plan with Sally to go to the writing festival in Penang, Malaysia.
* Sign up for guitar lessons.
* Spend an afternoon at the souk hunting for beads to make necklaces.
* Rip up my old magazines and make a collage about places I'd love to travel to.
* Reorganise the spare room so I have space to paint.

THE UPSIDE OF YOUR TRICKY TRAITS

You have conscientiously worked through 7 big Steps to become aware of, own, metabolise and create more space around your Tricky Traits. You have patiently unearthed layers of Tricky Traits. As you shone the light of awareness on some of your traits, you may have also glimpsed some of the gifts embedded within your difficult patterns. I have purposely avoided labelling traits as Negative Traits. If we label our challenging patterns as bad only, we split ourselves in two, good/bad, and we miss seeing the upside of some of our coping strategies.

One of my Tricky Traits is my overly pushy competitiveness. It gets me into trouble on the tennis court when I'm arguing about the score. It compels me to squeeze more physical activity into my schedule, and I get tired and grumpy, and I complain about the pain in my knees and wrist. But the upside of my competitiveness is that it fuels my enthusiasm to train for my games, to go to my physiotherapy appointments and to reliably show up for every game I commit to. My competitiveness can be annoying, but the upside is my enthusiasm and commitment.

Inside your Tricky Traits will be incredible resources and strengths. When we have more awareness about our traits, without compulsively acting them out, we can discern those strengths. For example, the Tricky Traits of control and manipulation also have within them the potential gifts of leadership, efficiency and attention to detail. Caretaking, a Tricky Trait we looked at in *Step 6*, has care, compassion and understanding embedded in it.

Choose five of your Tricky Traits and observe their upside. Use your journal or writing device and reflect on the resources and gems hidden within your Tricky Traits. Find those valuable kernels and celebrate them.

> ## Steve's story
>
> Steve did several sessions with me addressing his unfulfilling relationships with his wife, his father and his boss. He felt overwhelmed by his sense of duty to each of them. In pleasing each of these key figures in his life, he felt there was little time left to pursue his passions or Joy. But he wasn't too sure what his passion was – beyond making money and pleasing people.
>
> The eldest child of three, he had grown up with a domineering father and a passive mother. Steve was a smart child and received positive attention from his father by doing well at school and then at university. He was also good at sport, particularly athletics, and was recognised in his community because he won many athletic competitions. His father bathed in the reflected glory of his son's achievements.
>
> While Steve's mother enjoyed pottery and embroidery as hobbies, Steve's dad saw little value in artistic or musical expression. Being great at sport and successful at work was the purpose of life for Steve's dad. As Steve grieved the lack of true connection with his dad, he 'woke up to' all the hours he was dedicating to work in order to kowtow to his boss and provide for his wife's shopping habit. It became clear there was a part of him he had ignored, a part that wanted to paint. His elderly father didn't understand or encourage this. In fact, he was quite disparaging about Steve's first attempts at oil painting.

> But Steve pursued his desire and signed up for several series of classes at the local arts centre. His teacher, with whom he became good friends, encouraged him to exhibit his oil paintings at exhibitions at the arts centre and online. His plein-air painting trips have taken him to Florence, Bilbao and Grasse. He found a way to express a deep feeling side of his nature that he had ignored for decades in focusing exclusively on achievement. Connecting with his creativity and feelings has brought Steve a sense of peace, quiet Joy, and wholeness.

EMBODIED ECSTASY

Our Joy lives in and through our flesh, our very bodies. So many of us have troubled relationships with our bodies, judging them in cruel and harmful ways. The diet industry fuels this body craziness. Patriarchal religions have also made the body taboo and created horrible judgements around our naked beauty. Our judgements are harsh: "My body is not skinny enough, it's not muscly enough, it's not tall enough and it's too hairy," we lament. Or worse: "My body is ugly; it's shameful and it's evil."

The unhealed trauma that we may have received as children or later in life often ends up being dumped on our own innocent bodies. The inner critic can be vicious and unrelenting in its comparisons and impossible standards. In these ways, we separate our bodies from our hearts and also from our Juicy flow of Joy. The split leaves us starving for a loving connection with our bodies and the ecstasy that is possible when we allow ourselves to enjoy our physicality.

We explored the judgements and Tricky Traits we have in relation to the body in earlier Steps. But how can we reconnect to our Joy through the body? How can we move pain and stuck patterns out of our bodies? Movement and breath are two ways to connect with our embodied delight. We don't have to wait until we are ten kilos lighter, until we have completed the fitness challenge, the plastic surgery or until we are 'perfect'. Our bodies were designed to move and breathe. With moving and breathing comes feeling. Movement moves us out of inertia and connects us to our depths and our here-and-now Joyousness.

So how do you want to move? How do you want to move yourself out of inertia and into ecstasy?

Everyday ways I love to move and breathe

- On the tennis court
- On the padel court
- Yoga
- Running by the beach
- Walking
- Skiing
- Playing beach tennis
- Dancing

I'm not so particular about how I move, but I am deeply committed to moving my body in some way for at least an hour, six days a week. Your style of movement might be surfing, roller-skating or horse riding. How will you move and breathe with Joy every day?

Intentional ecstasy

There are times I choose to use a more intentional movement practice to bring awareness to a part of me that is feeling pain, frustration or confusion. I use these conscious movement and breathing practices to move Tricky Traits (particularly backed-up feelings) through my being. After an hour of one of these moving meditations (listed below), I never fail to land in an expanded sense of my True Self. These movement and breath practices work because they draw on shamanic practices that go back 75,000 years.

Your very being is organically connected to rhythm and flow. There is natural rhythm in your breathing, in your stride and in your waking and sleeping. In these practices you will remember you are connected to this infinite universe of constant motion. You may even disappear into the universe for a time as you play with these practices. In the disappearing beyond your usual time and space boundaries, you may open yourself to a whole new sense of delight and wonder in who you are discovering yourself to be.

Moving meditations

Here's a list of my favourite movement meditations. You'll recognise some of them from the 'embodied letting go' sections from earlier. Play with them and see which ones resonate for you.

* Osho Dynamic meditation
* Osho Kundalini meditation
* Chakra breathing
* Moving Cycle movement
* Five Rhythms dance
* Holotropic Breathwork
* Transformational Breathwork
* Hatha Flow or Vinyasa Flow yoga

The links for each of these meditations, which will guide you through the movement and breathwork experiences, are on my website (andreaanstiss.com/juicylife).

> "The oneness is gently and graciously available to anyone who wishes it."
>
> PLOTINUS

WHO AM I?

This is a fine question to ask and perhaps one that has been lurking in the back of your mind or burning in your heart. It's a question that may have guided you to this book. Or it may have lured you on a 40-year search to figure it out. It's the question that mystics, devotees, seekers and curious people ask. It's also the question we ask when we are fed up with a small, narrow life. Now that you are realising you are *not* your patterns, your trauma, your childhood conditioning or your ancestors' patterns, it's a good time to be curious about who you *really* are.

In my own childhood, my mum insisted my brothers and I went to church until we were 13 years old. After that, we were allowed to decide our own spiritual direction. As I watched the Anglican minister from my hard wooden pew, I was acutely aware that he didn't have the answer I was looking for. A year later another minister showed up, same rap, same black preaching robe with the stiff white collar. I knew he didn't have the answer either. The Nile River – where the baby Moses was left hidden in the bulrushes – seemed a very long way from New Zealand and frankly not so relevant to my young life. I was enormously relieved years later when I discovered Joseph Campbell, the American writer who wrote on comparative mythology and religion.

One of his most well-known quotes is, "Every religion is true one way or another. It is true when understood metaphorically. But when it gets stuck in its own metaphors, interpreting them as facts, then you are in trouble."

Through my ten-year-old eyes, I could see the efforts and the humanity of these earnest middle-aged male preachers, but their black-and-white approach concerned me. I needed a ton more answers. Mostly I needed *my* answers. And after years of exploring my truth, like most other seekers, I have a few answers and more questions.

As human beings, we need to bear the uncertainty of not knowing it all. We could call it riding the wave of uncertainty, but we don't just ride waves, we also ride circles, labyrinths, chaotic patterns, chronic patterns, Tricky Traits and hard decisions. We have ridden out years of Covid-19 – loss and dark nights – without knowing the end. Our courage is extraordinary! But our spirits and our nervous systems need support to help us bear all of this messiness as we walk through life.

Stillness

You have spent precious time peeling the layers off the proverbial onion. Those layers include the Tricky Traits and Trauma Traits that helped you make it to this point in your journey but no longer serve you. The onion skins include shame responses, boundary issues and other ancestral patterns you have faced. You've worked hard at self-reflection, are open to understanding and have compassion for yourself. You've conscientiously used the three inner steps of awareness, owning and action.

Now I invite you to sit in the stillness and drop deeper into your True

Self and the mystery from which it rises. In stillness, we can meet our multidimensional Juiciness and parts of ourselves that have been hidden. Stillness is the place where we can take time to integrate the journey we have been on. We catch up with ourselves. Resting or taking refuge in yourself is a smart way of receiving and assimilating the gems you have gleaned and of reminding yourself of your place in the universe. It's also a useful way of dissolving what you no longer need. And it's a sacred place of *knowing what you know*.

In stillness, we can simply be. It's the opposite of 'efforting' and aspiring. It's where we give space to our True Self and receive the grace of our existence.

One of my favourite meditations is the Osho version of Vipassana – because you can't do it wrong. Osho's version permits you to go off on a trail of thoughts; it's okay – just gently come back to your breath. In this version, all of your experience is included. Including everything creates spaciousness. This meandering mind, so easily taken by its stories, is invited to be met with gentleness.

My favourite ways to support myself to be still

Have fun experimenting with this list of ways to go inside yourself. Figure out what nourishes your stillness.

* Vipassana meditation – especially the guided Osho Vipassana meditation
* The third hour of a Holotropic Breathwork session, where there is space to integrate the first two hours
* Giving myself Reiki healing
* The MAGI Process from the teachings of Jason Shulman
* The Light and Sound meditation from Sri Gary Olsen

* Lying in the corpse posture or *savasana* at the end of any yoga practice
* Listening to spiritual music from artists like Krishna Das, Deva Premal, Nusrat Fateh Ali Khan and Omkara
* Listening to my favourite meditations on the Insight Timer app – in particular, Kristin Neff, Dr Megan Kirk Chang and Naomi Goodlet
* Sprawling on my couch in New Zealand with a glass of chardonnay in hand as I watch the sunset give the Remarkables mountain range a rose quartz crystal hue
* Lying or sitting next to a body of water – any beach, river or lake
* Looking at the stars in a place with no light pollution

Perhaps these suggestions have reminded you about what would help you to be still. Take your journal and reflect on what stillness practices you may want to try. Slow walking in the moonlight? Meditating in the desert? Floating in the turquoise ocean? Listening to the Dalai Lama chanting?

> "The Path of Love is really about belonging to this human family, to this extraordinary world with all of it... its challenges, all of its darkness and all of its light."
>
> ALIMA CAMERON

MORE THAN YOU HERE

You are already aware that you are wired for connection. No matter your age, your ethnicity, your religion or spiritual path, the gender you identify with, your sexual orientation, the political beliefs you hold and your socioeconomic background, you have a need to belong. We each need to feel included as a precious member of this human race. We need to feel welcome as part of this human family.

Much of our work has been about gaining an awareness of – and dismantling – the negative patterns or Tricky Traits you took on from those early connections and ancestors. This creates the space to see the goodness of the positive support you did receive. The movement away from entrenched family and cultural patterns that don't serve you and discovering what's nourishing for you is called *individuation*.

The power of community

As much as we need to individuate, we also need to *connect*. To thrive we need family, friends, beloveds, 'frenemies', mentors and community. For an ongoing awakening to our True Selves, we need a community of like-minded Juicy people or *sangha*, which means spiritual community. That community will ideally nourish us and challenge us to grow. In community, we learn cooperation and friendship. Kindness and respect are often values of spiritual communities.

I feel woven into some wonderful communities. I have my beloved family, extended family and inner circle of friends. I have my tennis community, which is full of Joy; it spans the UAE and New Zealand and it beckons me to the courts early most mornings to play, have fun, enjoy the wide expanse of blue sky and the meditation on a green ball. Then I often have a quick coffee with my sweetheart girlfriends before running to work. They are a solid community that fulfils my need for connection, affection and movement. I have a yoga community, which is fluid as I only go to class once a week in winter and more in summer. I'm connected to a broad spiritual community, made up of several organisations that weave and flow across the globe. That spiritual community is closely connected to my work. And finally, I have a precious writing community of writers that inspire and hold me accountable as I fulfil my writing desires.

Reflect in your journal about your needs for connection and community

- Where do you want to belong?
- What would you like to give to your community?
- What would you love to receive from your community?
- With whom do you want to spend your time?
- Who inspires and motivates you?
- Which clubs, groups or organisations feel inviting or Juicy to you?
- What do you want to learn?
- Do you want to give your time or support to any kind of mentoring or charity programme?
- Is there any unfinished business or Tricky Traits around the themes of competition, rejection, being a 'black sheep'? Or perhaps an aversion to receiving direction or feedback that can sabotage your desire to connect with community?

EVERYONE IS ACCOUNTABLE AND NO ONE IS TO BLAME

Bob Hoffman, the founder of the Hoffman Process, repeatedly used the phrase:

"Everyone is guilty and no one is to blame."

I prefer:

"Every adult is accountable and no one is to blame."

It's time to release guilt and claim our pleasure and power. Usually, there are emotions hiding under the guilt, and those emotions need an honest hearing. In fact, there is often profound sadness beneath the label of guilt. We know from Family Constellations that our parents and our grandparents were not to blame. Patterns get handed down from generation to generation, and those born generations later will carry the burden for the people that went before. Out of the need to win our parents' love and approval, we imitated them. It wasn't our fault; it wasn't theirs.

Accountability is fully possible as adults but not as children. Using our personal accountability empowers us to transform – one person at a time. It's the goal of Family Constellations, the Hoffman Process and most spiritual paths to help you accept your past and find understanding and compassion for your parents, so that you can connect to self-love and self-acceptance. In continuing to hold resentment towards our parents, we hold resentment towards life.

Forgiveness is a big word, full of promises of a clean slate, eternal peace and happiness. I love the idea in theory. It's the major teaching of Christianity and of the spiritual psychology self-study system *A Course in Miracles*. But forgiveness is the state we move towards organically *after* we've done the hard work of removing our blinkers and putting everything on the table. Before authentic forgiveness can occur, we need to do the 'eyes-wide-open' work of seeing both sides of the story. We must be willing to walk in the shoes of the other as well as express our anger, hurt and resentment in healthy ways. If we fail to do this and leap straight into an idea of forgiveness, with angels fluttering and trumpets blaring, we may be seduced by the *spiritual bypass*.

A spiritual bypass, also known as an *emotional bypass*, is where we skip over the messiness and inconvenience of owning and processing our emotions, in particular, the ones we label 'negative'. The anger, resentment and vindictiveness are pushed down where they poison our bodies or slip out sideways, sabotaging us and hurting others. This mechanism of repression and denial, which then leads to our darkness being projected 'out there' onto all the 'bad' others, is well described in the bestselling book *The Dark Side of the Light Chasers* by Debbie Ford.

TOWARDS UNDERSTANDING AND COMPASSION

I invite you to move gently and slowly towards understanding and compassion. And if you arrive there faster, then *mabrouk* or congratulations!

The Polish-Swiss psychoanalyst Alice Miller warned about the pressure to forgive. She writes in *Breaking Down the Wall of Silence*: "In my own therapy, it was precisely the opposite of forgiveness – namely, rebellion against mistreatment suffered, the recognition and condemnation of my parents' destructive opinions and actions – that ultimately freed me from the past."

You need to find your own way and move at your own pace. If you feel ready to open your heart towards others and yourself, you may wish to listen to a short compassion meditation adapted from the words of Buddhist teacher Stephen Levine. This meditation, simply called 'Compassion Meditation', can be listened to over and over again. If you would prefer to read it, the full text is on my website (andreaanstiss.com/juicylife).

Creating the mud that nourishes the lotus

In healing ourselves, we may have the illusion that we are getting rid of the parts of ourselves we no longer want. But in reality, the energy behind the parts that no longer serve us gets absorbed back into the Great Cosmic Recycling Bin – of which we are an integral part.

As you shine the light of awareness on your Tricky Traits, you may notice the old patterns you are ready to release will easily dissolve back into the greater light that holds us all. In Nondual Healing, created by Jason Shulman, we call this returning the *klippot*. The klippot are fragments of our being that have become disconnected from the whole. In stillness, we can feel these klippot and consciously let them go back to the light.

Other mythologies understand that our dross or heavy energies may be happily returned to the earth. And that the earth will gratefully receive the darkness we offer it. The dross of our Tricky Traits and Trauma Traits, including the dense stress and distress we hold in our bodies, is called *hoocha* by the Q'ero Shamans. The earth wants to absorb our hurt, pain and darkness according to ancient shamanic lore. Through shamanic meditations and shamanic-influenced practices like Breathwork, we can stamp, dance and breathe out our hoocha and spring clean our inner space. Our Joy has room to expand.

Our difficulties and our darkness provide the foundation from which we awaken. The Buddhists esteem the lotus flower, with roots latched into the muck and mud at the bottoms of ponds and rivers. No mud, no lotus. Thich Nhat Hanh, the wonderful Vietnamese Buddhist monk, reminds us that our personal mud and muck – made from our suffering – is needed to support the blooming of our compassion and loveliness. Our delight was never personal, for us alone. It is to be shared with the world.

TLDR TOO LONG DIDN'T READ

- (JL) Speak to yourself lovingly. Be a healthy mirror to yourself. Lest you forget, remind yourself you are an unrepeatable, beloved, totally precious being. You are lovable.

- (JL) Acknowledge and celebrate the positive gifts and inheritances you received from your parents and culture.

- (JL) Beyond your wounded child lives your wonder child – that part of you linked to your spirituality and creativity. How do you choose to express your creativity?

- (JL) Your body is wired to provide you with great Joy and ecstasy. Heal your relationship to it by moving it in loving ways.

- (JL) Stillness is a place you can drop into in order to integrate the journey you have been on. Take time to integrate your discoveries by going within to catch up with who you are becoming.

- (JL) Connect with friends and Deep Dive together. Create Juicy and caring communities to serve and explore what has value and meaning for you.

- (JL) We are each responsible and accountable as adults for our own journey through life. Releasing blame towards yourself and others sets you free to enjoy your life.

- (JL) Do what it takes to move towards understanding and compassion without skipping the steps outlined in earlier chapters.

- (JL) The universe is generous – it will recycle your dross if you let go.

MOVING ON

Coming to the end of this significant piece of work you have so courageously explored, you may wish to sit in stillness and reflect on the following questions posed by David Richo in his book *Shadow Dance*. They will help you become even clearer around the classic spiritual question, "Who am I... now?"

Six questions about your next steps

Consider these questions when thinking about what comes next:

1. What is behind me?

2. What is before me?

3. What are my griefs about what I am leaving?

4. What are my fears about what I am entering?

5. Who or what assists me in going on?

6. Who or what attempts to hold me back?

And finally... the power of a cosmic giggle

The story goes that when great masters get together, they laugh a lot. The degree to which we can laugh is connected to how well we can bear the chaos, absurdity, paradox and contradiction of our everyday lives. How can we delight in it all? The Dalai Lama is well known for his playfulness, jokes and gentle teasing. He says he is a professional laugher. Film clips of Bishop Desmond Tutu and the Dalai Lama getting together show these men cracking jokes and laughing uproariously. It may be that laughter is a universal index of spiritual development.

The best cosmic joke is that you already are what you are looking for. You are the love and the Juiciness and the fulfilment. It's already there in the very fabric of your existence. Your True Self has always existed. While laughter can sometimes hide sadness, wholehearted laughter is powerful in cutting through nonsense and the stories we tell ourselves. Laughing at ourselves and our crazy antics, as foolish human beings, is a particularly important skill.

Osho, a wonderful Indian spiritual teacher, continuously told jokes in his discourses. Many of them were highly inappropriate and often sexist. He said:

"Life as it is should be enough of a reason to laugh. It is so absurd, it is so ridiculous. It is so beautiful, it is so wonderful. It is all sorts of things together. It is a great cosmic joke."

When we can join the laughter, along with knowing it will all be over in the blink of an eye, we honour that urgency to enjoy each precious moment to the fullest.

And finally, as you reflect on your journey and embrace your True Self and Juicy Life, I leave you with an invitation from a great teacher of mine, Jason Shulman, the founder of The School for Nondual Healing and Awakening:

"Delight in all things."

RESOURCES

Books

Acknowledging What Is, Bert Hellinger & Gabriele ten Hövel, 1999

Aphrodite's Daughters, Jalaja Bonheim, 1997

Beyond the Brain, Stanislav Grof, 1985

The Biology of Belief, Bruce H. Lipton, 2005

The Body Keeps the Score, Bessel van der Kolk, 2014

Breaking Down the Wall of Silence, Alice Miller, 1993

Co-Dependence: Misunderstood – Mistreated, Anne Wilson Schaef, 1992

Codependent No More, Melody Beatty, 1986

Connected Fates, Separate Destinies, Marine Sélénée, 2022

The Continuum Concept, Jean Liedloff, 1975

Creative Visualization, Shakti Gawain, 1978

Daring Greatly, Brené Brown, 2012

The Dark Side of the Light Chasers, Debbie Ford, 2010

Dear Lover, David Deida, 2002

The Development and Evolution of Rebonding of the Body, Deanna Mulvihill, 2017

The Drama of Being a Child, Alice Miller, 1995

Dream Work, Mary Oliver, 1986

Dying To Be Me, Anita Moorjani, 2012

Eastern Body Western Mind, Anodea Judith, 2004

Eating in the Light of the Moon, Anita Johnston, 1996

The Examined Life, Stephen Grosz, 2014

Facing Codependence, Pia Mellody, 1989

Facing Love Addiction, Pia Mellody, 2003

Fat is a Feminist Issue, Susie Orbach, 1978

Getting Our Bodies Back, Christine Caldwell, 1996

Getting Rid of What You Haven't Got, Muktananda, 1974

Getting the Love You Want, Harville Hendrix, 1988

Healing the Child Within, Charles L. Whitfield, 1987

The Healing Power of Illness, Thorwald Dethlefsen & Rüdiger Dahlke, 1990

Healing The Shame That Binds You, John Bradshaw, 1988

The Hero's Journey, Joseph Campbell, 2014

Homecoming, John Bradshaw, 1990

How to Be an Adult, David Richo, 1991

I Am That, Maurice Frydman, 1973

Kabbalistic Healing, Jason Shulman, 2004

The MAGI Process, Jason Shulman, 2016

Mindful Aging: Embracing Your Life After 50 to Find Fulfillment, Purpose, and Joy, Andrea Brandt PhD, 2017

Movie Yoga, Tav Sparks, 2009

On Eating, Susie Orbach, 2002

Passionate Presence, Catherine Ingram, 2003

Poetry of the Spirit, Alan Jacobs, 2002

The Radiance Sutras, Lorin Roche, 2014

Radical Compassion, Tara Brach, 2019

Rebonding of the Body, Deanna Mulvihill, 1995

Romancing the Shadow, Connie Zweig, 1999

The Slow Down Diet, Marc David, 2015

Sweat Your Prayers, Gabrielle Roth, 1997

Substance Abuse Treatment, Deanna Mulvihill, 2017

The Way of the Psychonaut, Stanislav Grof, 2019

When the Body Says No, Gabor Maté 2011

Women, Food and God, Geneen Roth, 2009

You Can Change Your Life, Tim Laurence, 2003

The Zen Way of Counseling, Svagito R. Liebermeister, 2009

Articles

'9 Steps to Healing Childhood Trauma as an Adult', Andrea Brandt PhD, *Psychology Today*, April 2018

Websites

Andrea Anstiss
www.andreaanstiss.com

Aparajita Ghose
www.aparajitayoga.com

Christine Caldwell
www.themovingcycle.com

Co-Dependents Anonymous (CoDA)
https://coda.org/meeting-materials/patterns-of-recovery
https://coda.org/meeting-materials/twelve-steps

Cyntha Gonzalez
www.cynthagonzalez.com

Grof Transpersonal Training
www.holotropic.com

Hawa Breathwork Facilitator Training
www.andreaanstiss.com/hawa-breathwork-facilitator-training

Helen Wade
www.connect-wellbeing.com

Hoffman Process Australia
www.hoffmanprocess.com.au

Hoffman Process UK
www.hoffmaninstitute.co.uk

Hoffman Process USA
www.hoffmaninstitute.org

Jeff Foster
www.lifewithoutacentre.com

Jo Parfitt
www.joparfitt.com

Kali Martin
www.healingatthecore.com

Kas Ross-Smith
www.kasross-smith.com

Lisa Laws
www.lisalawscoaching.com

MayBritt Searty
https://maybrittsearty.com

Nacho Lopez Amenabar Medicine Man
nacholopezamenabar@gmail.com

Nondual Kabbalistic Healing
www.societyofsouls.com

Osho International Meditation Resort
www.osho.com

Pamela Wilson
www.pamelasatsang.com

Paris Williams
https://pariswilliamsphd.com

Path of Love
https:/pathretreats.com

Samar Ajami
https://www.rippleshc.org

Samar Ocean Wolf Ciprian
www.moon-yoga.com

Sharadha Bain
www.sharadhabain.com

Sofia University
www.sofia.edu

Terry Nathanson
https://terrynathanson.com

Tom Young
http://springcoaching.biz

APPRECIATION

Endless gratitude to my family, not least to Phil, my biggest cheerleader and my lionhearted partner in this long desert passage. To my children, Marcus and Perry: you are the best things that ever happened to me. To Beryl, my beloved and generous mother, who worked incredibly hard for all her children. In loving memory of Geoff, whose adventurous spirit I imbibed. To my four brothers and sisters-in-law: Michael and Pam, Craig and Julie, Digby and Bev, David and Donna, and my super smart and sporty nephews and nieces. I feel your love.

Huge thanks to Sharadha Bain: you were the steady boat! Deep appreciation to author and writing mentor Jo Parfitt, who didn't give up on me. Thank you to our beautiful writing group. I would not have fulfilled my dream without you fabulous three: Ruth Rusby, Susan Lane and Charmaine Saw. A deep bow of gratitude to Kas Ross-Smith for your wisdom and editing skills. And to Vanessa Arnold and Karen Henderson, who encouraged me and edited my early writing attempts.

Thank you to more of my sweetheart friends. To Samar Ajami for being the embodiment of unconditional love and luxe travel. Thank you Stephanie and Robin for so much, including the super yacht excursion to Ghantoot! *Obrigada* Manuela and Rob for the fun, fun, fun and the therapeutic sundowners. Thank you to our fabulous and enlightened tennis community for your precious hearts and sporty spirit – in particular, Beverly Constantinou and Gwen Tan-Sproule. You all keep me real, grounded and supplied with margaritas.

Thank you dear Beverley and Bob for providing the great food and snuggly bed for all the mid-winter visits. Thank you Elizabeth, Natalie, Annabel and Santi for welcoming me back home in NZ.

Thank you Cyntha Gonzalez for dancing with me in the Holotropic Breathwork and transpersonal paradigm. Thank you multi-talented Vanessa Arnold and Dr Yahia Kabil for all the beautiful Holotropic Breathwork Workshops we co-facilitated. And thank you Yahia for being a wonderful mentor. Monica Howden and Kali Martin, thank you for being my dear Capricornian sisters. Virginie and Kali, thank you for the Path of Love adventures.

Design beauties Aparajita Ghose, Niamh Kenny and Holly Wild, thank you – you have done a super job sorting out my website, insta and workshop promo. Thank you, Sonia Sfar for your gorgeous *Juicy Life* cover designs.

Thank you dear Sheila for sharing the Mama joys of Muscat and Dubai and always welcoming our family. Aum Shanti and Bharathi Ganguly, thank you for the sisterhood and the Sivananda Yoga.

Thank you to all my productive sisters. Mega thanks to Samar Ciprian for inviting me to share Holotropic Breathwork with your beautiful New Zealand community and midwifing the birth of Hawa Breathwork Facilitator Training. MayBritt Searty, thank you for your huge heart, talent with Family Constellations and generosity with our jungle adventures. Lisa Laws, thank you for our easy Inner Child workshop co-facilitation and my lush UK visits. Lisa Durante, thank you for your generosity in editing *Light Under the Abaya*. Deanna Mulvihill, thank you always for being an incredible mentor and for *Rebonding of the Body*. Aline, Jane, Ysanne and Susie, you were bright lights in my Riyadh transit; and Maureen and Dina, beacons in Bahrain; and Helen Wade, wonderful as my co-facilitator in the early Dubai days. Thank you to Ruth, Jami and Jan for my first-ever writing group escapades.

Thanks a million for our international Holotropic Breathwork Community, especially Stan Grof, Tav Sparks, Janet Kingsley and

Vicky Nicholson. Thank you also, Paulina Ulloa, for our short, sweet Dubai connection.

Gratitude to the Hoffman Process luminaries – in particular, Tim Laurence, Eliza Meredith, and Simon Matthews. Thank you to the ASOS community and beyond, including Jason Shulman, Brenda Blessings, Terry Nathanson, Dani Antman, Eef Gravendaal, and the De Poort souls.

Huge thanks to Kat McIvor, my wonderful mentor from the Institute of Transpersonal Psychology, now Sofia University.

Thank you to India and all the riches you've offered me over my multiple visits. And to my Osho Ashram/'spiritual Disneyland' teammates: Estelle, Lina, Sarah, Fernando, Stephanie, et al.

Radical gratitude to the people who took care of my home and children and allowed me to be the wanderlust therapist and teacher I am, especially Dhammika Godage and Lena Mendez.

And to Linda Sivertsen and the women from our BookMama writing workshop – thank you for the gorgeous Big Sur space and the inspiration. Much appreciation to editor Nancy Marriott of New Paradigm Editing and Writing, who helped me write my memoir, now morphed into this offering.

To my many clients and workshop participants through the years, a deep bow of respect and gratitude. Your precious hearts and trust in the process have inspired the structure and completion of this book.

I am awash with gratitude for all of you and all the beauty, light and challenges of these precious days.

ABOUT THE AUTHOR

Andrea Anstiss is a transpersonal psychotherapist, a certified Holotropic Breathwork facilitator, and a former Hoffman Process teacher with over 30 years of healing expertise. Her empathic approach helps her clients to heal the child within, to transform trauma, addiction and challenging relationships, and to awaken to their innate preciousness.

A resident of the Gulf States of the Middle East since 1990, she currently lives in Dubai and spends several months each year in New Zealand. Andrea works with her international clientele individually, in workshops and online. She creates a safe, nurturing space and facilitates the unfolding of her clients' deepest dreams, uncovering their hidden brilliance and transforming blind spots and wounds into potent resources.

With a seemingly unquenchable thirst for knowledge, Andrea has travelled around the world studying different therapies and healing modalities since 1983. She completed her Master's in Transpersonal Psychology in 2003 and was a teacher with the Hoffman Process UK from 2007 to 2013.

Andrea draws on a wide range of modalities with her clients. She offers both talk therapy and embodiment and energetic modalities, including Holotropic Breathwork, Nondual Healing and Rebonding of the Body. She has taught leading-edge personal development seminars throughout the Gulf countries, in the UK and in New Zealand. Andrea is currently offering Hawa Breathwork Facilitator Training for health professionals, therapists and coaches.

Andrea loves tennis, padel, yoga, and skiing. She is privileged to be the mother of two grown sons, and she relishes spending time with her extended family, drinking margaritas with her girlfriends and travelling for work and pleasure.

andreaanstiss.com

@AndreaAnstiss

Printed in Great Britain
by Amazon